CHIOS

OINOUSSES - PSARA

The fragrant island

EDITIONS
TOUBI'S ®
ΕΚΔΟΣΕΙΣ

© Copyright 1997   MICHAEL TOUBIS PUBLICATIONS S.A.
                    Nisiza Karela, Koropi, Attica, Greece.
                    Telephone: +30 210 602997, Fax: +30 210 6646856
                    Web Site: http://www.toubis.gr

ISBN: 960-540-233-5

Exclusive rights to Chios are retained by: "ANEMOS" Benettos Giannis - Galatoulas Giorgos S.A.
Chiou Karfa, Kondari, 82100 Chios. Tel.: 22710 22666, 22710 22780. Fax: 22710 81555.

"Beautiful island!
Your name alone
brings the sound,
of your flowered waters
and the rosebushes flowering."

G. Drosinis

CONTENTS

CONTENTS

The windmills, witnesses to the island's heyday and tradition, with the coast of Asia Minor in the background (Chora).

1 CHIOS

The island of mastic, jasmine and intoxicating fragrances, the island of orchards and orange groves, the noble island with its stone mansions and their pebbled courtyards, with its unique medieval villages and their towers. There is no other place like Chios in the Aegean. It is an island with an extremely old history which became a crossroads of the great civilizations, as it was one of the most important commercial depots during the Middle Ages and the Turkish occupation. It was also a great center of Hellenic spirit and intellect, the homeland of great teachers and authors including Homer, Adamantios Korais, Neophytos Vamvas, Yannis Psycharis, Alexandros Mavrokordatos, G. Theotoka, Emmanuel Roidis and Lambros Porfyras. Ancient sovereigns envied it, the Genoese fell in love with it and the Europeans were charmed by it from the beginning, as were even the Turks. It was extolled by foreign travellers but at some point the Fates turned against it. All those who have come to know it, admire it. Because its natural environment has remained pure and unspoiled, its climate mild, and its seas crystal-clear it is an island with a unique color all its own. Get to know it, enjoy it and open yourself to the unique atmosphere with which it is imbued.

Garden in Chios, color photograph by J.B. Hilaire (Benaki Museum, Athens).

Its inhabitants have remained uncorrupted,
optimistic, and light-hearted; you would
say they had been endowed by the natural
beauty of Chios itself with an incredible
desire to struggle on but also to look
at life from its good side. These people
welcome foreigners and offer what
they have with an open heart.
But Chios has a good deal more to offer
than just its beautiful beaches.
It has a complex personality with an impressive
number of special characteristics.
One by one they reveal their secrets to all those
romantics who like to ferret out old traditions
and cultures. As for the rest, it simply captivates
one with its authentic, colorful and comfortable
pace of life.

*The old, medieval villages of Chios, are full of picturesque
stone houses and covered alleyways.
Unique in beauty is Pyrgi with the famous "xysta"
ornamentation of its houses.*

In the medieval villages of Chios,
life is lived to another rhythm,
such as in the lovely village of Olympoi.

Nature and Location

The island's mild climate in combination with cool summers and the sparkling crystal-clear waters of the Aegean, not to mention the rich culture in evidence everywhere, attract more and more visitors each year. This sweet-smelling island of the Aegean runs to both tame and rugged landscapes and a visitor will find these alterations restful. The north side of Chios, the Voreiochora (the Northland), as it is called, has its own special kind of wild beauty. Sheer, towering, cliffs rise up from the sea to form Mt. Pelinaios, which is the highest mountain on the island at 1,297 m. The soil is rocky there and relatively poor.

The dense stands of pine which once covered a large part of this district, have been decimated by destructive fires. On the northwest side of the island, at Ayios Galas, there are caves which are interconnected Magnificent stalactites have been found there.

Traces of human habitation from the Stone Age have also been discovered in these caves which remain unexplored for the most part. The mountains get lower and lower as you move toward the center of the island, and the landscape becomes less forbidding, till one reaches the low, rolling hills to the south.

On the eastern side, near the town of Chios, lying between the mountains and the sea, is the largest and most fertile plain on the island, the so-called Kambochora (The Plains). The area is full of fruit trees, citrus for the most part. Enormous orchards of fragrant orange, lemon and tangerine trees, and further enhanced with almond trees, rich vineyards, and multi-colored gardens in riotous bloom inundate Spring with their intoxicating aromas.

That is also when the rare wild tulips come into bloom. From the middle of March to the end of April these so-called "lalades" sprout by the thousands everywhere: in the meadows, the fields and even on fallow bits of land, creating a unique spectacle.

Three kinds of tulip (Tulipa agenesis, praecox, undulatipolia) are similar, all being reddish. The latter is an especially rare variety of Chiot tulip which is noted for its spectacular white and purple flowers.

There are of course other rare wild flowers who have chosen Chios as their flowering place, such as the Persian cyclamen and certain kinds of orchids. Taken all together they create a magic carpet, a sumptuous feast of colors that each spring moves every visitor. Besides its wealth of flora Chios also plays host to important members of the animal kingdom such as the proud partridge. Formerly they lived by the thousands on the island and the villagers tamed them and raised them like chickens.

Today, in the nature of things, the fauna is slowly disappearing, but one still encounters quite a number of rare birds as they migrate from the north to the south and vice versa. Some of these birds are the so-called Turkoskatharis which literally means "Turkish beetle", the oriole and the Chionotsikla, the snow-thrush. In the southern section of the island there is a change in morphology.

The landscape consists of low hills which form small valleys between them creating the right conditions, unique in all the world, for the cultivation on the rare mastic tree of Chios. The "Mastichochoria" (Mastic-Villages) as they are called, is an area full of this kind of tree, which produces that fragrant resin so highly prized, the rare mastic.

In addition to the mastic trees in the southern and western part of the island, there are countless olive groves to be found with their abundant fruit.The vegetation is complemented by low Mediterranean shrubbery.

The island does not have a lot of surface water and there are only a few small streams, mainly in the north and central parts.

Rainfall is rare, especially in summer.

But it does have a great deal of underground water which comes to the surface in clear springs or is drawn up from wells.

In the northern part of the island, near the village of Keramos, the subsoil has rich deposits of antimony, which is minable.

Dotia, the most extensive mastic growing area, in the southern part of Chios.

Further on at Ayiasmata there are sulphur and iron medicinal springs. The coastline of Chios forms many beautiful beaches all around the island. They are all very clean, pebbled for the most part, and just the thing for a visitor who wants to enjoy the refreshing crystal-clear water and the enchanting underwater world.

It is obvious that nature has endowed this island more than most. The same is true of the weather. Chios is one of the sunniest places in the whole Mediterranean. Its climate is temperate, typically Mediterranean.

The summers are cool and pleasant because of the constant northerly breezes and the temperature does not exceed 28 Celsius. Furthermore, the winter on Chios is also gentle and mild with a temperature of 10 Celsius in the middle of January.

The glorious and attractive beaches that embrace the island and the wealth of the sea bottom revealed through dazzlingly clear water.

An island of the eastern Aegean,
Chios lies just off the coast of Asia Minor.
Only 3.5 nautical miles separate it from
Cape Pounda in Turkey and the peninsula
of Erythraia where Cesme is.
The island is located between Lesbos
to the north and Icaria to the south.
Chios has an area of 842 sq. km.
and a coastline 213 km. long.
The permanent residents of the island
number 50,000. The town of Chios,
the capital, contains approximately half
the population. The shape of the island
is long and narrow, moving from north
to south, and that is why Chios is also
called "Makri" (Long). The island is divided
into the Voreiochora, the mountainous
northern sparsely-inhabited district,
the Kambochora, the central, eastern plain
including the town of Chios and the rich
villages of Kambos, and the
Mastichochora, in the southern part
of the island with mastic trees and the
picturesque medieval villages of the
people who cultivate them.
The highest mountain on the island
is Mt. Pelinaios in the north at 1,297 m.
The most important commercial harbor
is in the town of Chios itself which soon
will be able to cater to private craft
as well. Smaller harbors can be found
at Marmaro in the northeast, near
Kardamyla, at Mesta in the southwest
and at Limnia in the west.
**The economy of the island is based
primarily on shipping, the production
of mastic and other agricultural goods
and to a lesser degree on fishing
and animal husbandry.**
Northeast of the island are a complex
of small islands, Oinousses, Passas,
Pontikonisi and Vatos.
Many prominent men of the sea
and shipowners come from Oinousses.
On the other side of the island,
to the northwest, are the islands
of Psara and Antipsara known for their
heroic exploits.

CHIOS

Alagatou · Eftichia · Agiasmata
enitourgia · Kourounia · Leptopoda · Agreliopo
Egrigoros · Lardato
Agio Gala · I Afrodissia · Keramo
Panagia Despina · Chalandra
809
Ielanios
Trypes · Potamia · Pispilounta
Parparia
Nea Potamia
Pirama
10
Agia · Markela · Moundon · Monastery
Volissos
Skariotis · Dievcha
Limnos · Lefkadia · Chori · Katavassi
Limnia

Viki
Kampia · Amades
PELINEO · EDELOS
Spartouna
1297
Fyta
Kipouries · MESSOVOUNO
OROS
1186
SKONI
Pitnous
NEFROLAKOS · Agios Issidoros · Agios · Georgios · Flori
MAGEMENA
PRASTIA · ELEOVOUNOS
Sidirounia
VOLISOS
Metochi · DIPOTAMOS
Anavatos
Agios · Issidoros
Elinta · Provatas
Avgonyma · Nea · Moni · Agii Pateres
Agios Markos

Giossonas · MARGARIT · Taxiarches
Nagos · Vlychada
Marmaro · KATO · LAKA
NAGOS
Amithountas · KORIPI
Kardamyla
DELFINI
KOUKOUDIA · Lagada · LANGADA · AGIOS STEFANOS
Agrelopos
Sykiada · PANTOUKIOS · Dachi
Pantoukios · Agios Ioannis · Tholos
Panagia · Myrtidiotissa · Mersinidiou
KENAVROS
796
18 · 643
KENAYROS
POS
482
Trypates
Karyes · Agios · Stefanos
Pefkonas

Vamvakas
Taxiarches
Evagelismos
Kastro · Oinousses
Marmaro
Spartounta
PONTIKONISOS

Vroulidia
Daskalopetra
Vrontados
CHIOS
Bella Vista

KORAKARIS
397 · KAMPOS
Lithi · KAKIA · RACHI
Dafnonas
Ververanto · Chalkio · Vassileoniko
Zyfias
Agios · Konstantinos · Agia Eleni
Karfas
Agios · Georgios (Sykoussis) · Vavili
Άγιος Γεώργιος · (Συκούσσης)
Sklavia · Neochori · Plakidiotissa · Thymiana · Agia Ermioni
Megas Limionas
Agia Fotini Beach
Agia Irini · Vessa · Tholopotami · Kalimassia · Agios · Emilianos
Merikounta · Meston · Limenas · Elata · Agia Fotia
479 · Myrmigi · Chalandrou · Messa · Didyma
Apothika · MASTICHOCHORIA · Exo · Didyma
Kataraktis
KRITHARIES · Kini · Vouno · Faxiarchis · Pagida
Mesta · ANTRAKLIA · Armolia · Patrika · Flatsia · Nenita · Vokaria
Olympi · Kalamoti · Ponta
Agios Minas · 259 · Lilikas · Gridia
Trachilia · Salagonas · Pyrgi · Agios · Georgios
Aghia · Dynami · 329 · Agios Ioannis
Kato Fana · MANOURAS · Komi
305
Emporio · KALAMOTI
Mavros Gialos
347
Dotia
Vroulidia

Airport ✈
Archaeological sites ⌷
Monasteries ⛪
Castle ♜
Caves ⌂

2

HISTORY

From Ancient Times to the Present

Ancient Times

An island in the Aegean such as Chios, so close to the shores of Asia Minor, and possessed of a temperate climate and fertile soil, could not help but attract interest very early on, starting in the Stone Age. This is verified by Neolithic finds from 3,000 B.C. which were discovered at Spilaio in the area of Ayios Galas in northern Chios. More recent finds from the Protohelladic period (2600 - 2000 B.C.) were found in the south, at Emboreio, while others from the Mycenean period were found at Fana and the town of Chios; they all confirm the constant presence of human life on the island for millennia. They also serve as proof of the historical myths which mention the first colonist of Chios as being Oinopionas from Crete, the grandson of Minos. It is said that he taught the inhabitants the art of viticulture and wine-making. One account says that the island took its name from the daughter of Oinopionas, Chiona. According to others the name Chios comes from the Phoenician word for mastic. Chios was also called Pityousa ("pitys" in ancient Greek meant pine tree) because of the large pine forest that covered its northern section, as well as Ophousa (Ophis = snake) for all the snakes that lived in its forests during antiquity.

Head of the Boston Kore (plaster cast), Archaeological Museum of Chios.

The first king of Chios was Amphiklos or Amphialos, who came there from Istiaia in Euboea in response to an oracle. A bit later the Ionians came from the coasts of Asia Minor and colonized Samos and then after a number of battles defeated the Carians and the Avantes who were living on the island and connected Chios with Panionion, that is, with the union of all the towns of Ionia at that time.

The town of Chios quickly assumed control over the rest of the island. Around the 7th century B.C. Chios developed into a major naval power and forged close links both commercially and culturally with the towns of Ionia. During that period the island flourished in every way. In all likelihood the homeland of Homer, Chios inspired the Homeric epic poets, who are thought to have been students of the great master. In the 6th century a school of sculpture was founded on the island by the renowned Mikkiadis, Archermos, Voupalos, Glaukos and others. During the same period the famous temple of Phanaios Apollo was built near the bay of Fana in the southern part of Chios. Its remains, today in the Archaeological Museum in the town of Chios, bear witness to the exceptional skill of its construction.

An exceptional example of Archaic ceramics from the cemetary at Lithis.

Around 600 B.C. what was known as the Great Covenant ("Megali Ritra") became law on the island, and established on Chios what was to be the first democracy in the world. It is said that Solon visited Chios and took many principles from its form of government for the institutions that he would later create in Athens.

The long period of peace, prosperity and progress were a blessing to the Chiots, the richest Greeks according to the ancient historian Thucydides. Their luxurious life took on proverbial dimensions and became known as "Chia Zoe" (Chiot Life), while their merry and happy-go-lucky character was called "Chios Yelos" (Chiot Laughter).

Chios never sought to establish colonies. Instead of that it created the so-called "emboreia" (trading posts) such as at Navkrati in Egypt. Chios itself was an enormous trading center, but

Depiction of the goddess Cy

alongside trade and transport it also endeavored to develop local production which included its famed wine and mastic, which was used as an ingredient in medicine.

But its prosperity was dealt a blow by Persian expansionism. The Persian King Darius replaced what had been until then benevolent despotism with harsh slavery and installed tyrants in the Ionian towns. With the outbreak of the Ionian Revolution in 499 B.C. the Chiots drove out the tyrant Strattis and with one hundred ships made a courageous stand against the Persians during the naval battle of Ladi. But the fall of the powerful Ionian town of Miletos changed the course of the war and led to the conquest of the island by the Persians in 493 B.C.

During the naval battle of Salamis the Chiots were obliged to fight on the side of the Persians. After the war and the defeat of the tyrant Strattis, Chios became a part of the Athenian Alliance. For quite a number of years it enjoyed its independence, experiencing a second period of prosperity owing to its correct administration, its naval power, and its trade and to the

...chaeological Museum of Chios).

tion of Chios and its turn toward Sparta. Subsequently the Athenians and the Spartans were at daggers drawn over who would have influence on the island, until the Antalkideio Peace accord was signed and the Chiots again became allied with Athens.

During the time of the campaign of Alexander the Great (334-331 B.C.) a Macedonian garrison was established on the island. Later, during the period of the Successors of Alexander the Great, the center of the Hellenistic world was far removed from the Aegean and Chios began to decline. Through the influence of Ptolemy I of Egypt, the island passed into the sphere of the Seleucids and Pergamon. It was subsequently occupied by Philip V of Macedonia and after the Battle of Magnesia in 189 B.C. it regained its independence. Around 190 B.C. the Chiots

many working hands of the slaves. Chios earthenware was renowned throughout all the world known at that time, and Chiot couches were famed for their fine craftsmanship and their luxury. During the same period the art of Letters also developed, being represented by two great writers in particular, Ion the Tragedian and the historian Theopombos. The Peloponnesian War dealt the island's prosperity another blow and Chios was on the side of the Athenians to whom it remained faithful until their defeat in Sicily. Thucydides gives a detailed account of the defec-

formed an alliance with the Romans and helped them overcome the Seleucids of Syria. Thus Chios acquired important privileges. During the wars with Mithridates Chios remained on the side of the Romans and because of that was destroyed. Sylla, however, in 84 B.C. defeated Mithridates and liberated the island.

During the early years of Christianity poverty and misfortune continued to plague Chios as on all the islands of the Aegean. There is little historical data for this period. Earthquakes and plague devastated the area.

Recently, during excavations near the town of Chios, a mosaic atrum floor from the Late Roman period was discovered which belongs to a structure.
It consists of eight scenestaken from the hunting of wild animals and gladitorial fights which are red geometrical motifs. The flexibility of the figures, the color contrasts and the realistic rendering of the motions make this an important work for the study of ancient art on Chios.

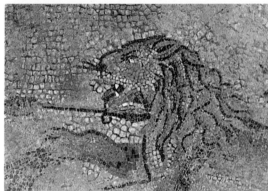

Impressive Roman mosaic discovered during the excavations next to Ayios Iakovos (St. James).

Byzantine Period

During the expulsion of the Christians by Decius in 250 A.D. mention is made of the island of Ayios Isidoros. The Early Christian churches of the 4th and 5th century which are found on the island are the only examples we have of some form of reorganisation. But the end of antiquity is signaled by the decline and the complete lack of data for the following centuries. Everything indicates that Chios followed the fate of the rest of Greece during the Byzantine period.

For centuries Arab pirates scourged the coasts and harbors of Chios, pillaging. Only after the recapture of Crete by the Byzantines did life begin to improve on Chios.

The Byzantines recognized the strategic nature of the site and fortified it. In the 11th century they built the town fortress for greater security. In the middle of the same century the famous Nea Moni (New Monastery) was founded under the guidance of the emperor Constantine Monomachus. Progress on the island continued despite the threats of the Turks and the Venetians.

Around 1204 Chios passed under the suzerainty of the Franks, just like Constantinople, but was later liberated by Duke Vatatzis.

By that time the Genoese had expressed their interest in the island, which was located on their sea lanes;they wanted it mainly as a commercial transit station for their Black Sea trade. Year by year the Genoese used more and more of the island as a station for their trips to the East. They gained ever greater privileges because of the assistance they offered to the emperor Michael Palaiologos against the Venetians.

The Genoese acquired their own public buildings, houses and churches and increased their influence on Chios. Meanwhile the ailing Byzantine Empire was unable to exclusively protect the island from the incursions of the Turks.

Thus, in 1307 Chios was handed over to the Genoese Benedetto Zaccaria and remained under Genoese rule until 1329. Then because of the violation of an agreement with the Byzantines, the island was reoccupied by Andronicos Palaiologos.

In 1346 the Genoese prevailed once more and held the island for more than two centuries. Throughout this whole period, Maona, a commercial firm in Genoa, governed Chios. Most of the members of Maona belonged to the Giustiniani family. They took over the economic resources and trade of the island as well as protecting it from its various enemies.

The governor, the so-called "Podesta", was appointed directly by the Republic of Genoa. There is a great deal of information to be had on this period from the archives in Genoa, as well as from the narrations of travellers.

The Giustiniani exploited the labor of the inhabitants to the utmost and frequently were very oppressive, particularly in religious matters, but they did organize the production of mastic and other products of the island as well as the security of the inhabitants in such a manner that Chios became the "Paradise of the East".

The interests they shared united the old Byzantine nobles with the new powerful Genoese families. The new, rich and effective class which was created, led to a new way of life which impressed foreigners with the prosperity it offered.

The standard of living and the cultural level of the period were both extremely high. Then the cultivation of citrus fruit and sericulture reached the island, that is the raising of silkworms for the production of silk.

The population of Chios increased, agriculture was put on a new basis, and the arts, especially architecture, flourished.

The Giustiniani managed to keep the island free from the Turks, even after Constantinople was subjugated, because of its intelligent policy and the significant tribute it paid to them.

Recently, during a series of excavations near the town of Chios, the mosaic floor of an atrium was discovered which belongs to a structure from the Late Roman period. It consists of eight designs primarily of scenes from the hunting of wild animals and from the arena, which are surrounded by five bands of black and red geometrical motifs.

*Rare icons from the ruins of the small church
of Ayioi Saranta at Thymiana.*

Around 1474 Christopher Columbus arrived
at the island on a trip to the east.
He disembarked at Daskalopetra
and was the guest of a Genoese noble.
Many historians maintain that Columbus came
to Chios for naval charts and to gather
information related to his great voyage.
In all likelihood he also chose Chiot sailors
as members of his crew. In any case, a number
of written sources indicate he stayed on the
island for some time and got to know
the value of mastic and the way of life
of the inhabitants. Many others believe that
Columbus himself came from Chios.
Even today there are families in the village
of Pyrgi with the surname Kolomvos.
Indeed there is an old coat-of-arms
on the facade of a house there which is said
to have some relationship to him.

Turkish Rule and Afterward

In 1556 Piali-Pasha occupied Chios without a
fight and dissolved the Genoese government.
But there were not all that many changes in the
life of the inhabitants or in production.
The residents retained quite a number of privileges and only a few Turks were living in the
castle. The local nobility kept its property,
its estates and its high position.
Chios flourished under Turkish rule, many
say because of the mastic, which they supplied
to the Sultan's harem.
The attempts that were made by the Florentine
Knights of Saint Stephen in 1599 and by the
Venetians (1694 - 1695) to take the island from
the Turks were fruitless. But at that time most of
the Catholic inhabitants of the island left.
The island experienced economic and cultural
prosperity throughout the 18th century.
Trade, mastic and light industry guaranteed
everyone the comforts of life and
on the other autonomy and peace were
favorable to the development of culture.
They had also learned to be realists
and to cherish progress. During that period
the School of Chios was founded and
it operated from 1792 until 1822.
Architecture reached great heights as a great
number of mansions and churches were built.
The population of the island increased and
approached 100,000. When the Greek War
of Independence broke out in 1821 Chios was
not involved at first. Then on March 11,
1822, rebels from Samos disembarked on Chios
led by Lykourgos Logothetis and together with
a handful of Chiots, headed by Antonis
Bournias, they besieged the Turks at the castle,
but without achieving anything.
On 30 March the Turkish fleet reached the island
under command of Admiral Kapudan Pasha
Kara Ali. The Turks landed thousands
of irregular troops with the sole purpose
of teaching the rebels a lesson. The rebels
retreated and the unarmed population found
itself at the mercy of the conqueror.

*"The Firing of the Turkish Flagship",
a work by Nikolaos Lytras.*

For fifteen days the Turks slaughtered, burned,
looted and destroyed all of Chios. The barbarity
surpassed anything known till then.
Many of the leaders of Chios were hanged
and more than 25,000 people lost their lives.
The rest were sold in the slave markets and only those
that managed to escape from the island were saved.
The destruction of Chios outraged the nations of Europe.
The French painter Delacroix depicted the destruction in
his famous painting which is exhibited at the Louvre.
From the general outcry over the slaughter, and under
the pressure of the Philhellenes, Sultan Bechit promised
to give a full range of guarantees to the Chiots to return
to their island. For a period he even funded their return.
In June of the same year Konstantinos Kanaris with his
fleet set fire to the Turkish flagship in the harbor
of Chios. In the great explosion the Kapudan Pasha
was killed. In 1828 the Frenchman Favreau attempted
to liberate the island but failed.
Starting in 1822 the Chiots who had escaped returned
and tried to remake their lives but conditions had now
changed. The scions of the old noble families and the
rich merchants who had held the economy in their
hands had fled and gone abroad. In 1850 a hard freeze
wiped out the citrus crop and agriculture was dealt a
very heavy blow. The earthquakes of 1881 destroyed
everything that had been left standing.
Three and one half thousand inhabitants lost
their lives. But slowly Chios began to reclaim its old
rhythm. On 11 November 1912 it was liberated
and became a part of the Greek state.
During World War II the inhabitants of the island resisted
the German occupation in every way possible.
Ignoring the possible danger they transported many
fleeing Greek and foreign soldiers to the Middle East
on small boats. Chios was liberated, along with
the rest of Greece, in 1944.
From wars and tribulation Chios suffered grave wounds
but it always held its head high. It may have ceased to
be a center for transit trade but it has kept its glory and
its love of culture. Today, due to its remarkable sailors,
its energetic merchants and its mastic crop,
it once more had a high standard of living.

"The Slaughter of Chios" (Eugene Delacroix).

3

CULTURE & TRADITION

Manners & Customs - People & Occupations
Arts & Letters - Architecture - Churches & Monasteries
Mastic and the "Mastichochoria"

Perhaps it was the good location of the island, near both the coast of Asia Minor and the Ionians and their rich civilization, or because it lay right on the commercial route to the Black Sea and the East. And perhaps it was also its excellent climate. But in any case, it is a fact that anyone who sank roots on Chios did not regret it. Its fertile soil, particularly to the west and the south, produced so many crops that the island has made itself self-sufficient from ancient times onward. Its inhabitants, despite the difficulties they experienced, managed to prosper throughout the larger part of their history. Thus, the Chiots developed a temperament that was cheerful and buoyant. Joyful and optimistic by nature, living on an island that possessed all the charms and advantages, they always found a way to enjoy themselves. Even during the period of the Turkish occupation, when the greater part of the rest of Greece was suffering under the Ottoman yoke, the Chiots, although working hard to pay heavy taxes, did have their own powerful form of self-administration and lived their life undisturbed for the most part. Thus they held on to their customs, their language and their religion unaltered down through the centuries. The Chiots created countless manners and customs in common, strong traditions which led to a deeper form of communication among themselves but also with their ancestors. At the same time, the economic prosperity of the island throughout the 18th century gave a great impetus to the arts and letters. On the one hand trade, mastic production and cottage industries insured the islanders their comforts while on the other autonomy and peace favored the development of culture. The experience of the inhabitants of Chios in their relations with foreigners taught them to be realists and to cherish progress. During that period they achieved great heights in architecture as a multitude of mansions and churches were built with features which were to lead to the creation of a completely original architectural tradition.

The "Aga" custom, from Mesta.

Manners and Customs

The major feast-days of Greek Orthodoxy were accompanied by a series of inviolate customs. Before the divine liturgy at Christmas, the home-owners made their houses spic and span in order to welcome the Divine Birth and they all asked for forgiveness from relatives, neighbors and friends before taking Holy Communion. The women made local varieties of doughnuts (loukoumades and a number of similar sweets) putting a coin inside one to bring good luck to whoever found it. The girls left their first fried doughnut half-eaten and put it under their pillow so they would dream of the man they would marry. During the early morning hours of Christmas Day, especially at Pyrgi, one person from each family, usually a girl, undertook to bring the holy water that insured the happiness of the household for the entire coming year. The one carrying it was not supposed to utter a word during this transfer no matter what happened, and thus the holy water was called "Amilito nero" (speechless water).

On New Year's Day the young men would visit all the houses singing local carols, accompanied by instruments, turning somersaults, playing pipes and bagpipes and ouds and eating from the festive tables. On that day everyone, especially the children, paid strict attention to their words and actions, because they believed they would set the tone for the entire year. Furthermore on those days amid the general gaiety that held sway, the skilled verse-makers made up so-called "painemata", that is, verses that sometimes praised but at other times teased and made fun of the leading families, the administration, neighbors and fellow villagers. These verses were always topical and usually original.

There were also a large variety of customs connected to Carnival, the days of hilarity preceding Lent. The most renowned Carnival celebrations in Chios were those at Thymiana with the famous Mostra which has been remained alive and well right up to the present and gives the holidays a special flavor. **Mostra** has deep roots which are lost in the depths of the Middle Ages. It is connected to the struggle of the Chiots against the pirates and marauders who in those times plagued the rich areas of the island, such as the village of Thymiana, which was so beautiful and renowned for its stone buildings. The final Friday before the end of Carnival the young people of the village would dress up in disguise, the Koudounatoi, literally those "with bells on". They would put on old clothes, often cross-dressing, hide their faces with improvised masks and act out little skits for the spectators. Then on Sunday they would all gather in the center of the village and to the accompaniment of instruments dance a special dance called **Talimi**.

This is a particularly impressive dance. It depicts the hand to hand battles of the villagers with the pirates, done in dancing movements. The masqueraders would split into two groups, one of which represented the people of Thymiana and the other the pirates, and then one man from each side would approach the other and they would meet in the middle brandishing long pieces of wood like a sword. Both sides always put up a stubborn showdown. This was followed by the next two dancers, opposing warriors, until it ended up by everyone getting into the battle. The group would also dance through the center of the village where they would take off their masks and perform the dance called the **"Detos"**. They would place their swords in the middle of the circle and holding each other by the shoulders dance around and around. Then singing a war song to the accompaniment of instruments they would head for the church of Ayios Stratis, their village church, where Chiot banners and flags were tied to the iron fence of the church.

Today this old tradition has been enriched with new elements, with satirical weapons and more contemporary attire. In any case the Mostra always starts the Carnival parade at Chora and all the Chiots gather there to enjoy it. They have always celebrated this three-day period of Carnival with their own special high spirits. At Pyrgi there was a special dance called the **"Diplos"** which was danced every Sunday before Lent except for the last one.

Traditional dances.
Above the "Talimi" and below, the "Detos", folk dances from the Mostra, a tradition at Thymiana during Carnival.

The dancers formed two rings which were identical to each other.
They danced in the main squares holding a candle since the dance started sfter dark This strange dance was done without musical instruments, with only the singing of improvised quatrains on various subjects following the main motif of the tune.
Every evening throughout Carnival the streets of the villages would be enhanced by the Carnival merry-makers. The young people formed small troupes and performed various comic skits outside the houses where the girls had gathered. Furthermore every Sunday the Acherades ("Straw-wearers") went out on the streets; they were men in disguise who would startle the girls decked out in all their finery by throwing handfuls of straw at them, causing disturbances wherever they went but a lot of hilarity as well.

Easter was always celebrated with great magnificence. On Holy Saturday, starting early in the morning, the young people would light fires in the countryside, the "lamps" of the Resurrection and sitting down around them boil eggs. On Easter Day there were great preparations made for the Easter table which included goat or lamb roasted over charcoal rather than on the spit, as was customary in most parts of Greece. Later the festival of "Niotritos" was established for eating and drinking outdoors. Thus from the beginning of Holy Week groups would go together and plan excursions to the sea where after the Resurrection on Easter Day they would eat, drink and celebrate until sunset.

On May Day, according to tradition, they all had to wake up very early in order not to be bewitched. At the crack of dawn the girls would pour into the fields and make the traditional May wreathes of fresh wildflowers. The young men, in line with a custom which came from the village of Thymiana, kept their strength for the evening. The whole night long they would go back and forth in the village snatching from the balconies and the courtyards

of the houses the most beautiful pots of flowers they could find in order to leave them at the door of their girl-friends. Because of that many people hid their potted plants on that day to keep them from being taken. The girls who found the most pots outside their door were very proud to find themselves so popular.

On May Day, right at dawn, a girl would take a jug and hurry off to get water, trying to avoid the sun and people, so that she would not be forced to speak to anyone until she had come back with a full jug. This was also called "speechless water". All the girl's female friends would be waiting for her at home and each one would drop some personal article into the jug, a ring, an ear-ring, a hairpin or similar objects.

The jug was covered and kept that way until the feast-day of St. John Klydonas, (which means omen or presage), on 24 June. On the afternoon of St. John's day the girls in the group would all gather again and the most proficient ones would recite an improvised quatrain, some of them serious, others flattering and still others teasing.

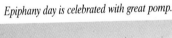

Epiphany day is celebrated with great pomp.

From the jug a first born boy would take out the so-called "rizikaria". After each recitation of a verse he would take out an object and give it to the girl it belonged to, who would then know the previous verses had been addressed to her. Thus the lucky ones were happy and the unlucky ones sad and subjected to teasing. One of the verses of praise from the Klydonas was:

> "Beauty in a person
> abundant charm.
> A young man that stands before you
> his wits will suffer harm."

One of the satirical Klydonas verses might have been:

> "You are far away and without charm
> and a boat patched with tar
> a magpie that haunts the beach
> who would want to be where you are?"

On the eve of St. John, fires, the so-called "Fires of Fana", were lit in the streets of the village and people would jump over them to exorcise the evil spirits and also trying to see who could jump the highest. This custom goes all the way back to antiquity and coincides with the summer solstice. With the strength of the fire they believed that people were purified, that they were delivered of evil and could thrive in their lives and be healthy during the new period of the year. On 15 August, the feast-day of the Virgin Mary, there were large festivals over the entire island. One of the most important was the festival at Pyrgi which even today attracts a great number of visitors both local and from outside. A celebration is held in the main square of the village, the so-called "green" and lasts the whole night with singing and dancing. The traditional dance of Pyrgi is danced at that time, one of the most interesting of Greek dances. It is a very lively dance with leaping steps and impressive turns and is danced by two men and a woman facing each other. The stalwart men and overall dynamism are the main characteristics of this rare dance:

> "We are the renowned men of Pyrgi
> our names written on cigarette paper."

As in every area of Greece, so on Chios marriage is the great event in the life of Chiot society and has always been the cause of great celebrations, dancing and feasting. It always started off with the engagement and this was done with the assistance of the matchmaker.

During that period love was not a seriously considered factor. What counted most was the family and the property holdings of the two families. So the engagement usually took place in the evening so it could be kept a secret and not be ruined by the envious or ill-wishers. That is why the lantern that the matchmaker always carried with her when she went out in the evening to the houses, became her symbol. The first official conversation between the two families was held at the prospective bride's home and dealt with her dowry and the economic situation of the prospective groom. When the assembled parties agreed on terms everyone was then treated to mastic sweets and wishes were made for a good start in life (to set down "good roots"). Part of the agreement was the setting of the date of the wedding itself and this involved a visit to the notary for the writing up of the dowry. The "Notaros", as he was called, had been appointed by the Turks in each village within the context of the local form of self-government common at the time. The dowry usually consisted of fields, various sizes of olive groves, groves of mastic trees, vineyards, clothes and other dowry articles such as Turkish coins. The prenuptial agreement also fixed the "deposito". This was the guarantee paid by whichever of the two parties broke the engagement. The amount of the deposit was fixed in accordance with the economic circumstances of each family. After the drawing up of the dowry agreement a date was set for the "filocheria" (kissing of hands) which always took place on a Friday. That afternoon the prospective bride would come to the home of the prospective groom accompanied exclusively by married women. The mother-in-law would put the rings on the hands of her son and the bride-to-be and then each of the parents, brothers and sisters and relatives would hang gold pieces on the new couple. Each time the couple would kiss the hands of the gift giver. So this ceremony came to be called the "hand-kissing".
The evening ended with the treating everyone there to sweets, and hand-made items in exchange for offering the couple many blessings. This whole process was called the anivasmata (the "rising") because it advanced the wedding process.

Then the songs and the quatrains started like the following one:

> "I will sing you a song of the chick-pea
> joy in the eye of the groom who chose his bride-to-be.
> Beautiful our bride and beautiful her dowry
> wonderful her group of friends who make her happy.
> A song I'll sing of the cherry and of this lovely couple
> who from youth to old age will be merry."

After the hand kissing ceremony, the prospective groom could freely visit the house of his prospective bride each Thursday and Saturday; that was considered obligatory and it was taken as a bad omen if he did not come. The young man would bring sweets or nuts with him. The couple was not left alone. They were always accompanied by a relative of the bride. If a crisis arose in the relationships between them the matchmaker would always hurry in to patch it up and to calm everybody down. If the agreement fell apart she had to return all the gifts from the hand-kissing ceremony to those who had gave them.

The preparations for the wedding began on the Sunday before the wedding when the future couple went to church and took communion. The next day, Monday, exactly seven days before the mystery of marriage would be performed, the bride's dowry was taken to be washed by her unmarried female friends, to the accompaniment of songs and best wishes:

> "Mario is doing washing in the river washing
> and rinsing it out again and it captures my mind
> Mario is washing her dowry washing it
> and making it white and driving me wild, red
> are her dresses rose-colored her aprons
> and everyone speaks of her charms
> and a young man walks beside her
> and takes her, takes her to the church."

Afterward the freshly washed dowry was laid out in chests, the number of which was used a measurement of the size of the dowry. On Thursday two girls, one from each family, would undertake the task of making the invitations and would go from house to house formally inviting the guests. On the afternoon of the same day the marriage bed was made, a custom that can be found in most parts of Greece. First the whole room was decorated, except for the bed. Then the girl friends of the bride, who had gathered there for that purpose, made the bed topping it with the "richtari", the lavish and expensive bedspread, and two pillows and everything that had been embroidered. Over the finished bed they would shower petals and rice so the couple would "take root". They would also set a small boy on the bed to insure that the couple would have a son. The parents, in their turn, would toss money on the bed as a gift but also for the prosperity of the new household, while the girls sang. The gifts came from everywhere until the wedding day on Sunday and they were all placed on the bed. The ceremony was usually performed in the church and more rarely at home.

The instruments, clarinet, violin, zither and lute, passed first below the bride's house:

> "Come out madam mother-in-law and bring the dove
> because the eagle has come to take her away."

The groom arrived at the bride's home with his own family. Then the bride would come out in all her wedding finery and the procession would set off for the church. This was always led by an unmarried girl carrying a tray with the wedding crowns and the "koufetes", the candied almonds, while to her right and left walked a boy and girl carrying large candles. They were followed by the musicians and immediately behind them the bride with her family and further back the groom with his relatives. At the ceremony two young people stood behind the couple, the best man and best woman, who could not be orphans. The young guests would take a bag of candied almonds from the tray and put it on their pillow so that they would dream of the one they would marry. After the ceremony, and back home the couple would offer everyone a drink of soumada (orgeat of almonds) and the candied almonds, with a drink of brandy or raki and a pastry and as they left they would receive a handful of candied almonds wrapped in a cloth. The groom was then called to the wedding table. The first dish was pilaf with the rendered fat from a rooster, in agreement with custom. The table was replete with all food imaginable. The wine flowed freely.

In the weddings at Pyrgi the whole village was invited to the celebration which lasted till morning and took place in the main square of the village.

Often when the newlyweds came from a poor family, the elders who ran the local government would place a tax on the inhabitants to pay for the wedding. That is where the well-known phrase: "Someone else always pays for the bride" comes from. The newlyweds were the first to begin the wedding syrtos dance:

"A song I will sing to you
about a lemon
long live the bride and groom
and the whole company.
A song I will sing to you
about a ten drachma coin
long live the bride and groom
best man and best woman."

The party would go on all evening and often until daybreak. On the day following the wedding, at midday, the in-laws would go to the house with "loukoumades" (kind of local doughnut) and other sweets. The first Sunday following the wedding the couple would go to the church to get the blessing of the priest.

After that final ceremony, their everyday life as man and wife finally began. Another characteristic feature of Chiot tradition is related to the **local costumes**.

The woman's costume is a particularly varied one and quite lavish for such a small place. The basic common features of the women's costumes are: a white chemise-like garment with embroidery on the hem of the skirt, a small blouse with embroidered sleeves and the "kamizora" or "samaraki" a kind of small vest with braces with many vertical pleats at the back. The everyday outfit included a blue or black sleeveless dress which came down to the knees. The most unusual accessory of the Chiot costume was the "stithopano" (breast-cloth) or apron or kerchief, a square or rectangular piece of fabric decorated with embroidery.

It was fastened at the top and fell freely to the abdomen. The most impressive part of the Chiot costume was the head-dress, the "sariki" or "papazina". This was wound around a hard base and its folds covered the head and neck. There was not much jewellery, usually just a bead necklace and that was worn primarily in Pyrgi.

Costumes de Chio. — Dessin de E. Bayard, d'après des photographies.

The men wore the island-style wide Turkish trousers, gathered between the knees, much like the ones worn on Crete. The basic elements of their costume were the shirt and over this the meïtani a double-breasted waistcoat. Around their waist they wound a long cummerbund of multi-colored silk which also had a fringe. In the town of Chios the official attire was complemented by a long cape lined with red felt and triangular pieces of blue velvet.

On the head was worn the indispensable red fez or a kind of black cap. On their feet the men usually wore leggings or gaiters, which were buttoned up behind the calf.

The Pyrgians, who had a more lavish costume, wore a gouneli over the kamizora, a heavy woven woollen waistcoat. In the Philippos Argentis Folklore Museum, which is housed in the Korais Library, there is a rich and impressive collection of Chiot costumes and weavings from many parts of the island, which is well worth the visitor's time.

People and Occupations

For many centuries the people of Chios were occupied mainly with farming. Already in ancient times, according to tradition, the island produced a famous wine from its vineyards in the east and south.
Many writers referred to it, from Aristophanes to Athenaios in the "Deipnosophistae".
Viticulture continued to flourish during Byzantine times until it was restricted during the Turkish occupation.
The orchards of Kambos during that time of intense cultivation had an enormous production of citrus fruit and exported it to many areas.
Today the well-known tangerines and almonds of Chios continue to be grown. The age-old olive trees on the island produce tasty olives and a fair amount of good quality olive oil. There is still some limited cultivation of legumes as well as fruit trees and the miniature tomatoes of Pyrgi which are cultivated without water. When picked they are usually tied in bunches and hung outside like onions.
Their skin dries up but the inside stays juicy for a long time. Even today one can still see these tiny, delicious dark red tomatoes hanging on the balconies of Pyrgi.

Farming was done on a more restricted scale in the 18th century after the earthquake and the freeze destroyed the largest part of the crops. A lot of time and effort was required for agriculture to recover and it never did reach its previous level. The inhabitants preferred to turn their interest to shipping, a profession that was dangerous but also profitable. Thus with the passage of time more and more Chiots turned to the sea, creating a powerful maritime tradition from which many modern day shipowners have come. Indeed, half the population of Chios today is involved with sea transport and communication and there is constant development

The only exception to a general decline in agriculture is the production of mastic which even though it too has been limited, still employs a significant segment of the population in the southern part of the island. Every year around 100 tons of this rare and quite expensive product is produced and exported throughout the world. Of the many light or cottage industries that existed in the past, today only the production of certain, "spoon sweets", as they are called, is still in operation, particularly in the town of Chios. Aromatic and without additives, a holdover from another period, they are made of preserved oranges, baby eggplant, cherries, grapes and many other fruits and vegetables. In addition one finds the sweet pies, almond cakes and various sweet drinks, including the renowned fruity Chiot liqueur, as well as Anthonero (literally "flower water") and rose water. Other wealth-producing sources for Chios are marble and the reddish brown stone from Thymiana. Fishing continues to be a steady form of employment for some. The waters around Chios are rich in the finest quality fish and sea-food and they are in great demand. The Chiots have kept the old tradition of pottery making right up to the present, manufacturing decorative and useful ceramic items. Silk was another important product of Chios. At the beginning of the 19th century the yearly production reached thirty thousand okes. In the 18th century there were as many as 1,200 workshops for the making of silk brocade gold and silver thread. Their products were exported to the East and were in great demand for their quality. The highly-skilled craft of Chiot embroidery and weaving is still carried on by the women of Kallimasia, who have their own local Women's Cooperative, as well as in Thymiana and other areas. Tourism is the modern occupation that has shown the greatest development in Chios in the past few years. Many travellers visit the island, primarily during the summer months, and along with them come the Chiots who have been scattered all over the world.

Arts and Letters

The cultural contribution of Chios to Greece, particularly in the 17th and 18th century, was extremely important. The high standard of living gave an impetus to the growth and development of a distinguished and very rich culture. On the one hand there was the powerful bourgeois class of merchants and scholars, of Korais, Mavrokordatos and Neophytos Vamvas, while on the other there was the strong traditional element kept up by the local people, and this led to the creation of a very distinctive culture.

Within the climate of the humanistic Enlightenment and in tandem with the economic prosperity of the island under the Turkish occupation, before the outbreak of the Greek War of Independence of 1821, the famous School of Chios was founded in 1792 and operated until 1822. Eminent teachers with an international reputation taught here, as well as researchers into the local culture.

One of the most brilliant of the teachers and the director of the school was **Neophytos Vamvas** (1770-1856). Vamvas learned his first letters on Chios. He was a student of Proios and Athanasios Parios.

Later he went to France and there joined up with his compatriot and another great scholar of the period, Adamantios Korais, and he supervised many of his works. In 1815 he returned to Chios and assumed the directorship of the school. During his tenure, Greek, Latin and Turkish were taught along with mathematics, painting and music. It also operated as a printing shop where many writings were published for the students, as well as a large public library.

During that period it also awarded scholarships to Chiot students to continue their studies abroad and then to return to their homeland and teach at the School.

After the destruction of Chios, Neophytos Vamvas became a monk and taught in many of the higher schools of Greece, such as the newly founded National University.

Vamvas is considered to be one of the promoters of the sciences in Greece. He wrote Rhetoric, Elements of Philosophical Ethics, Syntax of Ancient Greek and many other books as well.

Other important people in letters came from Chios. Among them was **Adamantios Korais** (1748 - 1843) who offered so much both to Greece and to his own birthplace, Chios. He is considered one of the most important scholars to emerge in modern Greece and one of the most illustrious representatives of the Greek Enlightenment. He played a major part in the uprising of the Greeks against their Turkish conquerors and helped safeguard the intellectual tradition of Hellenism during the time of subjugation. Korais came from a family of prosperous Chiot merchants and grew up in a patriotic environment. He had a broad education. In his youth he lived in Europe, studying foreign writers and philosophers. A stalwart defender of Greek Orthodoxy without being either a fanatic or a pedantic formalist, he was condemned by the clergy for his liberalism. For a long period he lived in France and starting in 1796 devoted himself to to the struggle for the Revolt of the Greek nation. He wrote "Brotherly Instruction" urging the people to rise up and later "The Warriors Song" exhorting the French to come to the assistance of the Greeks.

Later Korais turned his attention to education. He proclaimed that his compatriots would only achieve liberation when they learned to read and write, when they acguired a knowledge of the treasures of Greek antiquity.

His offering was major, and introduced ancient Greek writers to European scholars as well. In 1805 Korais began his monumental work.

The "Greek Library", gathering together the important works of many ancient writers. With this work, Korais achieved international recognition. He also contributed to the publication of a Greek dictionary.

Other important Chiot scholars came from the Mavrokordatos family. Alexandros Mavrokordatos and his son Nikolaos were also to provide inspiration in behalf of the preservation of the Greek spirit during the Turkish occupation through their works and their good offices.

Today the famous Korais library in the town of Chios, contains besides his own personal library valuable documents and his letters. The library has a precious collection of over 135,000 volumes. The center of the intellectual and cultural activity on the island is at the Omireio (Homeric) Cultural Center of the Municipality of Chios. It was built by the Chiots Michalis and Stamatia Xylas. Every year many important cultural events are held at the Omeirio, events which go beyond the confines of Greece and take on international dimensions.

Of the arts, architecture and hagiography have made major advances in Chios.

The mansions of Kambos, the houses of Kastro and the medieval villages in the south of Chios are of exceptional interest.

Many foreign travellers have described in glowing colors their impressive and unique characteristics.

The prosperity that Chios experienced for a long period favored the development of this art. But the churches of Chios also have their own personal style. An exceptional example of Byzantine architecture and a monument to Christianity is the main church of Nea Moni ("New Monastery"), and most of the later churches on Chios were built to its plan.

The icon-painter Chomatzas was a Chiot, one of the most important members of the Cretan School. A part of his work still survives in the church of the Panayia Krinas ("Virgin Mary of the Lily"), in the village of Vavyloi. Another superb icon-painter was Konstantinos Katarrachtis, a genuine representative of the folk technique, who had his own original and daring style. Works of his have survived in good condition at the Mounda Monastery in northern Chios.

The island has seen well-known sculptors at work in more recent times. Yannoulis Chalepas and his father carved the iconostasis of Ayios Loukas (St. Luke) in Varvasi. It was of grey and coral marble. At the end of the 19th century another sculptor, Georgos Bonanos, made the tomb of Michael Zygomalas, a column with his statue and in front of it the figure of a little girl sitting on the prow of a ship.

In the Public Gardens of Chios is the bronze statue of the heroic figure from the island of Psara, **Konstantinos Kanaris**, done in an exceptionally realistic manner in 1922 by Michalis Tombros. Works by Thanasis Apartis, "The Unknown Sailor" at Vrontados and "The Captain" at Kardamyla, are distinguished by their inner force. Their stance and their expression are full of a particular vitality. Near the main entrance to the Korais Library is his statue, which was done by Yannis Pappas at the beginning of his career (1938-1940).

Furthermore, at the Commercial High School stands "The Teacher" a work by Konstantinos Klouvatos. In the town of Chios, at the Turkish Baths behind the Town Hall is the National Gallery of Chios which has works of important modern painters.

Architecture

*An island with a flourishing culture such as the
one on Chios would naturally have its own
distinct traditional architecture. Thus, starting in
the 14th century and continuing for the next five
hundred years, Chios developed a personal
architectural style which distinguished it both
from its neighboring islands and the villages
on the coast of Asia Minor. Unfortunately, an
enormous part of this architectural wealth was
destroyed in the 19th century, in the terrible
earthquake that devastated Chios. Despite that,
some of the remaining buildings and certain of
the building complexes still give us the chance
to conduct our studies and even to admire the
important architectural phenomenon of Chios.
The architecture of this island even changes
from one end to the other, with dramatic
differences between the northern and the
southern parts.*

*Generally speaking, we can distinguish three
main units of architectural activity: Chora
and Kambos, the Mastichochoria and the
Voreiochoria in the north. All three of these units
have a host of typological, morphological and
structural differences which are due, on the one
hand, to the natural environment itself but also,
for the most part, to the prevailing economic
and social conditions of the corresponding
areas. Thus in the capital of Chios, Chora,
as well as in the broader district of Kambos,
one can observe an architecture reflecting
prestige, which is adapted to a commercial
bourgeois society, with important western
influences. Old Chora developed down through
time, just like any other medieval village:
the construction of the castle - the extending
of the settlement – the transferring of
commercial activity outside the walls
– and the building of new fortifications.*

*Mansion in Kambos made
of the famed Thymiana stone,
full of the charm and romanticism of the past.*

The houses that were erected in line with this development were built in the rowhouse system which was made necessary by the narrow confines of the space.

Thus, the mansions of Chora have only one free facade, lack courtyards and have developed upward to a height unusual for that period three storeys. The living spaces communicated directly with one another via doors which were approached by an internal staircase which set off from the main entrance on the ground floor. At the same time, the ground floor was used for a number of auxiliary purposes, as a shop or a storeroom. Furthermore, the kitchens or the servants quarters were housed in the main dwelling but were served by a secondary internal staircase. But despite all the elements they have in common, the grand houses of Chora did not strictly adhere to any type because of the host of additions that were made down through time, as well as the wide variety of floor plan.

Conversely, the mansions of Kambos, which for the most part were used as country dwellings by the rich merchants of Chora, were arranged typologically more for the display of architectural forms than for functionality.

Here, behind the stone courtyard walls and the severe entrance arches, were two or three storey houses with a view open on all sides, large external stairways and spacious courtyards with the traditional cistern and well.

The stairway, the "tsardi", a space used for summer living, the archways and of course the enormous orchards with the flowering citrus trees, are elements that are to be found in Kambos but are missing in Chora.

Above: Ruined mansion in Kambos.
Below: Ayios Eustratios at Thyminana, one of the largest churches on Chios.

In later years all these tendencies were influenced by the culture of the Ottoman empire principally, on a decorative level. Thus, were fashioned the houses in Chora and Kambos with their monumental character; unfortunately the style was adulterated in our century by the addition of a mishmash of new features.

On the other hand, the Mastic-Villages followed their own separate architectural course. The main role in this series of events was played by the special historical nature of the area which was directly connected to the production of mastic. The insuring of the valuable monopoly on mastic and the need to protect these villages from pirate attack led to the construction of powerfully fortified settlements which were clearly indebted to the Genoese.

These villages, which as a rule lie in small valleys, far from the sea, characterized by a dense urban tissue and by four-sided defensive walls, which are formed by the facades of the houses at the edge of the settlement.

In the center of the villages, sometimes in an enclosure with four corner turrets, was the defensive tower, the largest structure in the village which was used as a last resort of refuge in the event the village was captured by enemies. The fortress-like character of these settlements, however, is stressed even more by other details: the absence of trees, the small dimensions of the public spaces, as well as the extending of the living spaces over the streets in the so-called "votes".

As for the houses in the medieval villages, they consist as a rule of a ground floor and a second floor which communicate by means of an interior staircase. On the ground floor were the storerooms, and auxiliary spaces, as well as the stables, for reasons of security, while the living quarters were on the second floor.

This is where the atrium was found, a space which made for ease of movement, and supplied ventilation and lighting as well as allowing direct access to the flat rooftops. These flat roofs all on one a level, are a unique feature of these settlements, affording the potential for the inhabitants to move from one house to another throughout the whole village in the event of an attack.

Another characteristic of these villages are the skepasta ("covered areas") the rooms that were developed over the semi-circular arches which joined opposite rows of walls on the narrow streets. In any case, the most impressive architectural feature of the Mastic-Villages are the "xysta": these are a technical peculiarity and an impressive pictorial element of facade decoration with geometric and natural motifs. These were done to preserve the idiomorphic feeling which characterizes, even today, traditional settlements, such as Pyrgi, though they have their roots centuries back, during the time of Genoese rule.

The **xysta** constitute an important institution in the Mastic-Villages, one which spread to others areas of Chios as well, ornamenting both churches and houses.

Going from the southernmost to the northernmost tip of Chios, you come upon radical differences. In the north the mastic tree was not favored and farm land was limited. The inhabitants, who lived almost exclusively from farming and animal husbandry, were used to a poor, humble life without any material demands. Thus the design of their settlements is in essence primitive, based on a pure form of folk architecture of primarily folkloric interest.

The only architectural and historically important feature is the existence of majestic towers at the center of the villages, a basic point of similarity with the Mastic-Villages, but which cannot be studied in depth because of a lack of data.

Despite that, the basic architecture as well as the structural logic are common in both cases: the application of highly crafted methods, such as the use of carved stone for the ostentatious self-promotion of the wealthy.

Details from the unique "Xysta".

The dwellings, built of local materials, consisted of a ground floor and a second floor which respectively house animals and people, while at the same time they were relatively separate from the rest of the settlement.

It is characteristic that entire families lived and slept together in a single space, on a slightly raised wooden platform, near the fireplace. In only a few cases, such as at Kardamyla and Ptyos, does one find arches or vaults which are imbued with a modicum of the architectural magnificence of Chora.

In general, the architectural forms of the north are practically non-existent, since they were made to serve their poor origins and structural needs. Despite that, certain of these villages have been kept in good shape right down to the present, and are of especial touristic interest.

Because of that we must mention Anavatos, in the central part of the island, which historically was designed as a military bulwark to survey the deserted western coasts and to give warning of a surprise attack. Practically deserted now, but untouched by the passage of time, Anavatos is a unique example of the natural fortification of the villages found during that period, which made them practically invisible and unapproachable to any conquerors.

Anavatos: the Mistras of the Aegean.

Copperplate of Nea Moni, by Th. Weber.

Churches and Monasteries

Christianity reached the island early, as antiquity waned. The new religion fortified its faithful with piety and forbearance. This is where St. Isidore, St. Merope and St. Marcella were martyred. Since then many, many churches and monasteries have been built on Chios with many different architectural characteristics that are different from those in the rest of Greece. Most of those that have survived are copies of the famous Nea Moni. This monastery lies in the center of the island at Provateio mountain and is one of the most important monuments of all Christian Orthodoxy as well as the most important site on the island. Its architecture and mosaics place it among the most important churches n Greece. It is a rare example of the advanced artistic ideas of the 11th century. This is an imperial church of the highest Byzantine art which was built by the Byzantine Emperor Constantine Monomachus with the contribution of Theodora the Great in the 11th century.

With the very first glance even the most ignorant visitor will be impressed by the church of the Theotokos (The Mother of God). Its daring architecture is the prototype of the elegant island octagonal variety. The huge dome stands there imposingly. Through the high windows the light bathes the area and gives life to all the saintly figures which have been there on its walls for hundreds of years. You imagine them moving and looking at you with their stern ascetic eyes. The half-destroyed mosaics still suggest the distinguished art that went into them. The marble iconostasis has been dominated by the miracle-working icon of the Virgin Mary for more than 900 years. On the floor can still be seen the drawings and the symbols of the five "loaves" on the priceless marble slabs. The entire atmosphere in this holy place is imbued with the awe of human beings in the face of so much holiness, inspiring one with a sense of wonder and exaltation.The inexpressibly lovely Byzantine art of Nea Moni became the model and source of inspiration for a great number of the churches of Chios, all of which, however, have kept their own unique characteristics, representing the genuine tradition of Chios. Among them the Panayia Krina ("The Virgin Mary of the Lily") stands out; it lies just outside the village of Vavyloi. This church is an exact copy, in miniature, of the main church of Nea Moni. Of particular interest are its wonderfully crafted wall paintings.

Scattered throughout the island are countless churches and monasteries, witnesses to the deep religiosity of the inhabitants. One of the most noteworthy is the church of Ayioi Apostoloi (The Holy Apostles); and the small church of the Taxiarch (Archangel) at Pyrgi, Ayios Georgios o Sykousis (St. George the Sykousian) at Zyfia, the Mounda monastery in northern Chios and the Panayia Ayiogalousina at Ayios Galas. There is also the Monastery of Ayia Marcella to the west, near Volissos, the Panayia Sikelia (The Virgin Mary of Sicily), the Monastery of Ayios Minas outside of Neochori, as well as the tiny very old church of Ayios Georgios and Ayios Isidoros (St. George and St. Isidore) in the town of Chios. It is also worth paying a visit to the church of Ayios Eustratios in Thymiana, the Monastery of Ayioi Konstantinos and Eleni (Sts. Constantine and Helen) at Frangovouni, the Panayia Plakidiotissa at Kallimasia and the Panayia Agrelotou near Kalamoti.

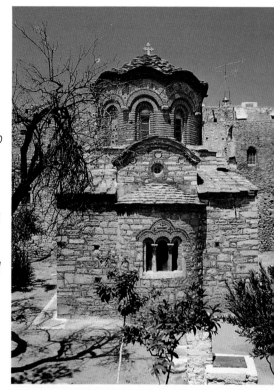

The picturesque little church of Ayioi Apostoli (The Holy Apostles) at Pyrgi.

The Monastery of Sts. Constantine and Helen at Frangovouni.

Mastic and the Mastic-Villages

The plant that makes the flora of Chios unique is the mastic tree and its sap. It is a low tree, almost a shrub, with spreading branches and an ash-colored trunk, either light or dark depending on how old it is. It also has irregular scales, like wrinkles, like a pine tree.

From these oozes the natural resin, the mastic. It appears that it has been known since antiquity for its medicinal properties.

It is mentioned by Pliny, Dioskouridis, Galen, Theophrastis and others.

This unique, noble and very expensive product which is produced exclusively on this island and is indissolubly connected to the history of Chios. For a very long time the Chiots owed their social prosperity to the mastic tree.

It is not known precisely when its cultivation became widespread. But tradition has it that the mastic shrub began to weep when St. Isidore was martyred by the Romans (250 A.D.) Indeed it has been shown that the Chiots began to systematically cultivate the mastic tree around that time.

The highly unusual climatological conditions in south Chios have created the perfect environment for the mastic-producing tree: an exceptional amount of sunshine year round, little rainfall in the summer, a mild winter with temperatures that never go below zero degrees Celsius as well as the composition of the land which is made up of limestone formations which do not hold a lot of moisture on the surface.

The cultivation and processing of mastic is still done today in the old traditional way. This requires many working hands, time and effort, something which makes mastic even more precious.

The jobs involve the tapping of the of the trunk, and the tapping and the collection of the mastic takes all summer and has many stages. During the preparations the ground is cleared and smoothed under each tree.

Mastic collecting

The trunks are cleaned and scraped and swept down. Then the ground is spread with white earth, particularly in areas with red soil. The white soil is easily separated from the mastic during cleaning. Then there are a number of other technical processes for the preparation of the mastic tree, followed by the tapping with a special needle or a small hammer which demands great skill. The bark of the trunk is slit into vertical or horizontal sections, the so-called kenties , to a depth of 2-4 mm. being careful not to expose the bone of the tree. Each tree is tapped 5-8 times with a few kenties which always start low down on the trunk.

The mastic begins to flow from the slits and it takes about 15 days for it to thicken and be ready to collect. The first gathering of the thick mastic takes place around the fifteenth of August. Then there is the second tapping and the final collection around the middle of September.

After the entire production has been gathered the processing of the mastic begins. First there is the sifting, called the tachtarisma in the local dialect, and then the mastic is washed with soap, that has no impurities, and cold water. It is spread out to dry and then is scraped with a small knife piece by piece to be cleaned of any foreign matter that may have stuck to it. This is the so-called pinching .

The final sifting through a different kind of sieve is done to separate the mastic into qualities and kinds, chunks, fine pieces and their by products. Today mastic has many uses.

Its most widespread application in chewing gum and as a flavoring in confectionery shops and distilleries. Essence of mastic is basic to high quality lacquers f or furniture and musical instruments.

It functions as a stabiliser of colors in textile factories and painting. In perfume factories it is an ingredient used in the various formulas for perfumes, f acial creams, nail polish and so on. In addition it is used in orthodontics and medicine and has a very wide range of application.

The trade in mastic was efficiently organized by the Maona, the share holding company which belonged to twelve merchants and ship owning Genoese; the name comes that from the Arabic "Maounah" which means a commercial enterprise.

The difficult "kentima" process used for the mastic harvest so the mastic will flow from the tree trunk.

The owners of the Maona were called the Giustiniani perhaps from the Giustiniani Mansion in Genoa which was the headquarters of their firm. The Genoese distributed mastic throughout the Mediterranean, to Genoa, Greece, Alexandria, Cyprus, Rhodes and Syria and all the way to Constantinople. During the Turkish occupation the Turks permitted its free trade requiring only that they receive 26 tons from every harvest in lieu of taxes. Later the Chiots took the trade over from the Franko-Levantines. The Mastic Producers Cooperative was founded in 1938.

On the south coast of Chios where the mastic tree flourishes, there were 27 villages which were called the Mastichochoria or the Mastic-Villages, since that was where the mastic cultivators lived. The historical starting point of the villages was during the period of the Byzantine empire, but they became a major force during the period of the Genoese occupation.

The Genoese were the ones responsible for the fortress-like form and the fortification of the Mastic-Villages, both for reasons of defense against ambitious would-be conquerors and for the control of the valuable monopoly in mastic.

Then, when Chios fell under the domination of the Turks, the government of the Mastic-Villages passed into the hands of Aga Sakiz Emini, who focused his interest on the maintenance of the monopoly in mastic, imposing severe penalties on smuggling, but at the same time guaranteeing very favorable living conditions for the inhabitants. Thus the inhabitants of the Mastic-Villages, even though they could not enjoy even the smallest part of their natural wealth, did not have any problems under the Turkish occupation.

But nature itself treated them badly. With the catastrophic earthquake of 1881 all of the southeastern villages sustained major damage. Today there are 24 Mastic-Villages left, some of which are still in very good condition, the most important and largest being Pyrgi. Others are Mesta, Olympoi, Kalamoti, Armolia, Kallimasia, Nenita, and Vessa.

Through sifting the "tears" of mastic are collected and left to solidify.

Chora, as the town of Chios is called throughout the island, is built in the middle of the eastern coast of the island, facing Cape Erythraia on the mainland, indicating its close bonds with Ionia and the shores of Asia Minor during ancient times.
To be more specific, it lies on the narrowest passage to the northern Aegean and Constantinople (now Istanbul). That is why its geographical position was of such supreme importance for many centuries and has never changed since. Despite the fact that the location of ancient Chios is not precisely known, because there have not been a sufficient number of excavations, the archaeologists place it within the boundaries of the present town. Finds from the southwest side of Vounakiou Square and the cemeteries indicate the existence of a large, flourishing town which is mentioned by Herodotos, an Ionian town with an enormous harbor large enough for 80 ships, a theater and a large temple dedicated to the goddess Athena and an enormous marble statue. It is thought the harbor lay in front of the garrison, while the walls ran all the way down to the coast. There were two cemeteries discovered, one at the site called Rizari and the other at Kofina. The first belongs to the Geometric period and the second is dated to the end of the 7th century B.C. The town was inhabited at least until the end of antiquity as can be seen from the finds from Early Christian churches in the same area. But very little is known about the Byzantine period.

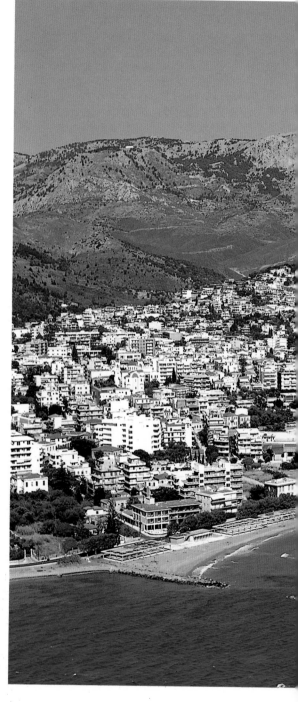

Aerial view of the town.

OF CHIOS (Chora)

Later, the nucleus of the town s development became Kastro (The Castle) which for many years was the administrative center of the island. But gradually, during the early years of the Genoese occupation, the so-called proasteion (literally, suburb) began to be created, a new settlement outside the walls.
The main road, the Aplotaria, set off from the harbor to fill the needs of commerce and is already being mentioned by 1555, while Voukaniou Square is first mentioned in 1639. During this period and the Turkish occupation, Chios was referred to as a wealthy and pleasant town bustling with activity and three-storey stone houses that were reminiscent of Genoa.
It was the period of prosperity when even the settlements outside the Castle were fortified. The nobles also kept a second residence in the countryside in the area of Kambos where living conditions were more pleasing.
Then there came the slaughter of 1822 and the earthquake of 1881. The town was almost completely destroyed. Only a few ruins remained of the settlement that had so impressed every traveller in the 18th century. The more recent town acquired a different character. Large churches and neoclassical houses with influences from Smyrna opposite gave it a new flavor. Today, despite constant demolition of the buildings, the town is endeavouring to preserve its refined architectural environment, which is what made it unique. The older elements coexist with the new such as in Vounakiou Square, a few meters from the center of the harbor, which is framed by new administrative buildings, cafes and an old mosque with its tall minaret. It is there that the **Byzantine Museum** is housed today.

The minarets of the mosque that today houses the Byzantine Museum and the marble fountain of Malek Pasha, two of the many sights in the town.

From the Early Christian and Byzantine period have survived a collection of architectural members and pottery, of great importance f or Chios, as well as rare sculpture from the early Italian Renaissance. Three of these pieces, which have been preserved practically intact, were the lintels of the entrances to wealthy homes in Kastro and are from the 15th and 16th century.

There is also later sculpture, influenced by western ways of thinking along with Turkish and Jewish tombstones with inscriptions, all housed in the Museum of Chios.

Near here, toward Aplotaria, on Michalou St, you will come upon the **Archaeological Museum** of Chios, with finds from the Stone Age. The oldest exhibits are of ceramic vases and pot shards. Very little has survived from the great output of sculpture but what has, are examples of exceptional technique revealing the grace of the Ionic style. There are also finds from the Roman period, as well as a very important stele with the letter of Alexander the Great in which he decreed the change in the form of governmens turning it from an oligarchy into a democracy and announcing the return of the exiles.

On the north side of Voukaniou Square is a simple column with the names of the notables of Chios who were hanged on that spot by the Turks in 1822.

A little further on, at the beginning of Martyron St. there is a large stone Turkish fountain from 1768. It is square and has a wooden roof and an arch with a double curve on each side, and is a noteworthy example of baroque (1730-1808) which was prevalent in Constantinople.

Above: The column with the names of Chiots who were slaughtered in 1822.
Below: Old fountain in Voukaniou Square.

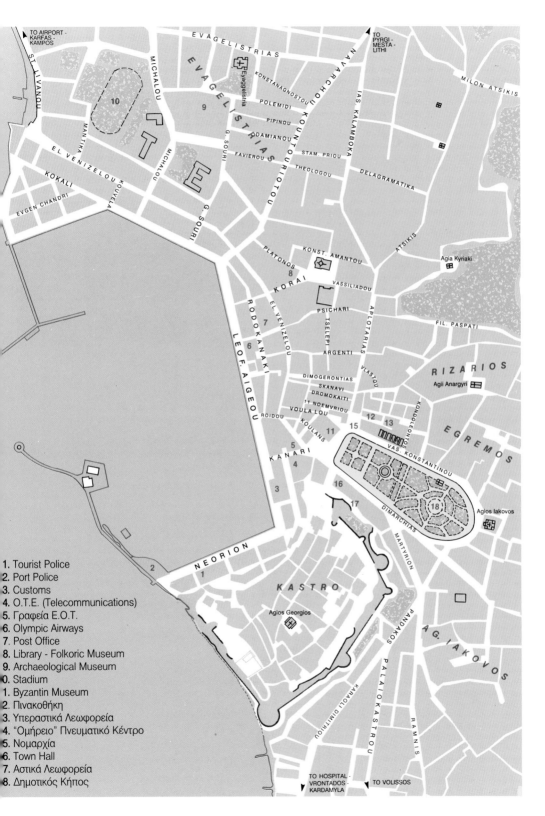

1. Tourist Police
2. Port Police
3. Customs
4. O.T.E. (Telecommunications)
5. Γραφεία Ε.Ο.Τ.
6. Olympic Airways
7. Post Office
8. Library - Folkoric Museum
9. Archaeological Museum
10. Stadium
11. Byzantin Museum
12. Πινακοθήκη
13. Υπεραστικά Λεωφορεία
14. "Ομήρειο" Πνευματικό Κέντρο
15. Νομαρχία
16. Town Hall
17. Αστικά Λεωφορεία
18. Δημοτικός Κήπος

The Castle

The town s Castle (Kastro) played an important role, both in medieval and more recent times. It was the center of the political and military administration. It covers approximately 400 square meters and was originally built by the Byzantines for the fortification of the town around the end of the 10th century. The walls that survive today have undergone many changes and attempts at reinforcement by both the Genoese and the Turks.

The Giustiniani used the Castle as their base of operations, and the Catholic Bishop lived there, as well as the Greek nobles. Unfortunately, the towers, the palaces, and the churches which all the travellers of that period mentioned greatly impressed have not survived. Information exists on important Italian civil engineers and artists who were invited there during that period to decorate the buildings inside the Castle of Chios.

Today the Castle contains the old Ottoman settlement, with small houses and narrow alleyways where once only Turks and Jews lived. The street plan has not changed for 300 years but catastrophes and earthquakes were the direct cause of the renovation of the houses while the works in the harbor at the beginning of the century changed the look of the Castle. The southern section was pulled down and the moat was buried under the landfill.

Lately there has been an attempt to salvage and restore the Castle. The main entrance (Porte Maggiore) lies on its south side near Voukaniou Square, behind the Town Hall. It is in three parts and the passage turns twice; there is a covered gallery that forms a vault. The gate is protected by a circular tower which was built by the Venetians. The level area that comes after the exit from the gallery is dominated by the reconstructed Giustiniani Mansion, the administration building in late Gothic architecture with large vaulted spaces which was built of local porous sandstone. Today it houses the Giustiniani Museum with treasures from Byzantine churches, Early Christian mosaics, Byzantine and post-Byzantine wall-paintings and wooden sculpture.

On the same level area is a large square room covered with four pointed groin-vaults.

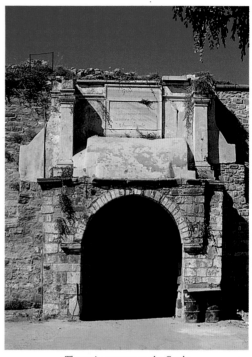

The main entrance to the Castle.

It is built into the wall and its use until 1822 is still unknown when it was transformed into a dark dungeon . It was here that the notables of Chios along with the Metropolitan Platon were held for 40 days before being led to the gallows by the Turks on 23 April 1822. A little further north in the next flat area, you reach the Turkish cemetery where i n the confine of a small courtyard stand the marble tombstones of eminent Turks.

Here lies buried the Kapudan Pasa Kara Ali, the leader of the Turkish fleet that was burned by Kanaris on 7 June 1822 in retaliation for the slaughter on Chios.

The tombstones in the cemetery are of artistic and historical interest.

The reliefs are brilliant examples of Ottoman art which took elements from baroque and has many similarities with 19th century Greek folk motifs.

On the main street, to the left are the ruins of small mosque, the Batrakis mosque, which was built over a Christian church. Continuing along the same street you will come upon the church of Ayios Georgios (St. George).

Section of the castle walls.

This was built around 993. A Byzantine church, and then a large Genoese church, it was turned was also turned into a Turkish mosque in 1566.

The main street ends at the north corner of the Castle where to the left you can see the Turkish baths and the spherical domes which was built in 1700. From the flat roof of the north circular tower, the open sea can be seen in all its grandeur. From there you can make out the sea wall, the north tower and the moat.

This tower was known as the tower of Antonio Zeno and was rebuilt by the Venetians in 1694. The Zeno Tower was built in accordance with the fortification needs of the period when large cannon were used, and had a complete defensive system with a parapet on the roof, ports for cannons at the base and interior communications for the soldiers.

In the interior of the building there is the Krya Vrysi (Cold Fountain) which is a large half-basement reservoir for water with a roof of groin-vaults supported on eight pillars.

Originally water was drawn up from a vaulted gallery which extends along the entire length of the east side of the building.

Later it was fashioned with a low fountain on its southeast side. Despite the fact that the vaults seem to indicate Genoese origins for the monument, in all likelihood it was built by the Byzantines.

Kechri, a small church with ancient masonry and bricks, is also considered to be the remnant an old Byzantine building. A little further south Koules rises up, a massive Turkish tower from more recent times. There is evidence that another earlier Genoese tower was built on the site, known as Senta, and an arms-depot.

The towers and the walls of the Castle can be made out better from the exterior side. The materials that were used were uncarved or square stones, limestone, the hard rock of Thymiana or the grey stone from Fokaia. The tower next to the main entrance was the most important one. On its flat roof is where the nobles appeared during the period of Genoese occupation to speak to the mass of the people who had gathered in the commercial square. In the next tower to the west can still be made out the escutcheons of Genoa and the Giustiniani with the date 1425.

The Moderne Town

Leaving the tower you return to Voukaniou Square, the center of the town, with its enormous plane trees and many cafes. From there Aplotaria Street, the historical main commercial road of Chios, sets off toward the south. This road has the heaviest traffic in the town and there are all kinds of shops here where the modern merchandise is found side by side with perfumed traditional "spoon sweets", the fragrant mastic and the famous ouzo. Its name is owed to the old merchants who came here and "spread out" (aplonoun) their wares to show them to prospectve buyer. This area is full of narrow parallel lanes which lead from all directions to the center. A few hundred meters further on you unexpectedly come upon the religious and spiritual center of the island. The Cathedral of Ayioi Viktori (Sts. Victor), which was built after the earthquake of 1881, dominates the area. A bit further on is the famous High School of Chios, a well-cared for building with neoclassical architecture and a long history. It is a successor to the famous School of Chios which was founded in 1792 and operated until the destruction of the island in 1822, during a period when the rest of Greece was still struggling under the Turkish yoke. The economic power of Chios and its autonomy in regard to the Turks led to a strong current of intellectual and cultural development. In 1832 the School began to operate again and brilliant teachers of the period taught there, such as A, Parios, Theodoros Proios, Neophytos Vamvas to name but a few. Practically opposite the High School of Chios is an equally imposing neoclassical building that houses the Korais Library, one of the largest and most noteworthy in Greece, with more than 135,000 volumes.

The building housing the Korais Library which is also home to the Argentis Ethnological and Folklore Museum.

The library s old building was a part of the School. After the bombardment of 1822 it was rebuilt and contained the private library of Adamantios Korais (3,500 books), many of which contained his own hand-written notes.

Among them are priceless editions from the campaign of Napoleon in Egypt.

The **Argentis Ethnological** and **Folklore Museum** is housed in the specially fashioned second floor of the Korais library.

It contains an exceptionally representative collection of local costumes and many embroideries from every village on Chios.

Weavings, copperplates, very old carved wooden implements and tools, as well as historical paintings and portraits of notables from the private collection of the Argentis family, take the visitor back to the atmosphere of that period.

Besides Voukaniou Square and the Aplotaria one of the most vital parts of the town is the harbor.

A multitude of restaurants, snack bars and cafeterias lend a joyous note, day and night, drawing travellers and locals to the pier.

Another tourist area on the south side of the town, with intense night-life is the coastal **Bela Vista** which contains modern hotel units, restaurants and bars with all night entertainment. Leaving the town and heading toward Karfas, four kilometers away, you reach the Ionian swimming pool, an important modern installation which indicates the concern of the Chiots for their youth and for athletics.

The town of Chios has a fraternal relationship with the town of Genoa in Italy to which it is connected by many ties.

This initiative belongs to a series of activities of the citizens of Chios to preserve the traditional architecture of the island.

Night view of the harbour of Chios.

Kambos

To the south of the town spreads out the fertile plain of Chios which is known by the name Kambos. An idyllic area, unique in the Aegean, it is dense with orchards and citrus groves. Kambos has a great deal of underground water and the most fertile soil on Chios. It is full of fields and the magnificent summer homes of the old aristocratic families of Chios.

Travellers from the 18th and 19th century have described the beauty of this area.

Going down the countless narrow and winding lanes of Kambos one is impressed by its two and three storey mansions. Built by and large out of the superb stone of Thymiana with its impressive reddish earthen color, they are surrounded by high stone walls with imposing courtyard gates which with their arched entrances have a grandeur all their own.

Behind the severe facade is hidden a different, more pleasing world. A large courtyard with a finely crafted pebbled floor, under the cool shade of the trees, lavish flower gardens with long alleys and arbors, the wheel-well for watering and the marble cistern covered with a pergola and a grape vine. And among them a large mansion with two or three floors, with a double external staircase which goes up to the first floor and a superb view over the trees.

The ground floor of the dwelling was used as a storeroom or a place for the farm equipment. Frequently from the interior side of the stone walls rose up enormous, thick cypress trees which served to protect the sensitive citrus trees from the wind and the private life of the nobles from the prying of the outside world.

Kambos began to be inhabited by the Maona and the local nobility around the 14th century. It is calculated that at one time there were over 200 estates there but only a few still survive from the mansions of that early period.

Despite that Kambos retains its old glory and through its atmosphere is able to transfer the visitor back to the romantic days of yore. Today many owners of the mansions are carefully restoring them to their original form, of the first or second stage after 1881.

Several of them have been made over into lovely traditional inns.

The most noteworthy mansions which have survived in excellent condition, and representative of the architecture of Kambos, are the Kazanovas or Mermingas mansion, the Mavrokordatos Lekana at Frangovouni, the Zygomalas and the Kaloutas. Furthermore, the best preserved building is that of Philippos Argentis on Argenti St. It has been largely restored since 1937 and gives you the clearest picture of how the old mansions of Chios looked.

Details from the impressive gates and the majestic mansions at Kambos.

5

SOUTH-EAST CHIOS

Karfas - Ayia Ermioni - Mega Limnionas - Thimiana - Nehori - Agia Fotia - Kallimasia - Katarraktis - Komi

Welcome to the cosmopolitan region of Chios. The whole east and south sides of the island have been under rapid tourist-related development. This is where the most recreational facilities are located and which they can respond to the visitor's highest demands. Supermodern hotel units, apartments, pensions, rented villas and single rooms in the idyllic environment of the south-east coasts are available for comfortable vacations. The exquisite sand-beaches of Karfas, Megas Limnionas and Komi are the friendly hosts of every visitor offering access to many marine sports and recreational activities. As in most beaches of the area, there are restaurants and taverns serving tempting delicacies, fresh fish and seafood specialties. Day and night there, life is intense and joyous. The scenic little coves of Agia Ermioni, Agia Fotia and Katarraktis with their quiet pebble beaches give a different dimension to the landscape.

Even in the hinterland the villages have something special to offer. There is plenty of sightseeing on that route. At Thimiana do not miss the great church of Agios Eustratios all made from the famous Thimianousian stone. It is also worthwhile to adore from up close the monasteries of Agios Minas in Nehori and Panagia Plakidiotissa in Kallimasia. Here is where your acquaintance with the picturesque Mastic-Villages begins. These are medieval village-fortresses with unusual fortifications, built to protect the mastic-producers from the violent raiders of that era. Among them are Kallimasia, Nenita and Kalamoti, all worth visiting. The tranquil landscape of rolling hills which we traverse on our way south is complemented by countless groves of the rare mastic-trees as well as lush olive-tree groves, fruits-trees and vegetable.

Karfas - Ayia Ermioni

South of the city of Chios, following the coastal road past the airport and Kontari with its many clubs and restaurants, we arrive at cape Fragonisi. This suburb is the site of **Ayios Konstantinos ke Eleni's** (Saints Constantine and Helen) convent, founded in 1898 by Saint Pachomios. Here the strict rules of monastic life are still observed; entrance is forbidden to all males. It is said that many miracles have taken place in this nunnery.

In 6 kms we get a glimpse of Karfas, the most touristically developed area of the island. It is possible for its name to be a derivation from the homeric "karfaleos" meaning arid, dry. True to its name, **Karfas** is unblest with any springs, but it is endowed with one of the island's most beautiful beaches. The wide shoreline stretches for about a mile and the thin sand makes the crystal sea waters sparkle like emeralds.

The seaside is shallow, thus very friendly to little kids. In recent years the transformation of Karfas into a tourist resort has been very rapid and today the small cosmopolitan town bustles with life day and night. Here one can find luxurious hotels as well as single rooms to let. Plenty of restaurants, taverns and stores serve the vacationers round the clock.

Leaving Karfas the shore road, scented by the fragrance of mastic and thyme, passes through Plaka - famous for its viticulture since the Genoan occupation and arrives to Ayia Ermioni; this is a handsome community with an age old history and a small cove with fishing boats anchored right next to a 1700 built chapel. **Ayia Ermioni** is also becoming a rich resort with beautiful houses, pensions, neat hotels and stores.

Megas Limnionas - Thimiana - Nehori

A little further down lies another Chian small resort especially leeward to north winds, **Megas Limnionas**. There, a beautiful pebble beach invites the traveler to cool him-herself in its quiet waters. A long line of taverns and outdoor restaurants complete the picture. Going uphill to the hinterland, we come to **Thimiana** an old village with rich and ancient history.

Its first appellation used to be Euphemiana meaning famed place. It is the locale of many quarries bearing the Thimianoussian stone, the famous red and brown porous rock.

Constructed with this stone are the

1., 2. Karfas' cosmopolitan beach.
3., 4. Megas Limnionas
   5. Agios Eustratios at Thimiana
   6. Nehori

mansions of Kampos (Plain), many Chios' churches and buildings on the Asia Minor coast opposite. Visitors of **Ayios** (Saint) **Eustratios** church at Thimiana can admire this uniquely Chian characteristic.

The church is one of the largest on the island built in a neo-byzantine style and made wholly with thimianousian stone.

Thimiana is situated at the feet of two hills and comes from the union of three medieval settlements. Today it is one of the most populated communities of the island.

Much interest presents the local Halloween custom, called Mostra, because it combines the village's history with pagan elements continuing a very long tradition.

Here is also the convent of **Ayioi Anargiri**; built circa 1639, it used to have many visitors who were mental patients seeking cure by the miraculous powers of the two healing saints. Legend has it that the number of the monastrery nuns was always 28; if it was to get any higher, then some nuns would unexpectedly die. The convent ceased to function in 1987. Today there are plans to reopen it as a seminary for clerics. The village next to Thimiana going south is **Nehori.**

A new village as its name indicates, it boasts for its main church of Panayia (Virgin Mary), a valuable piece of local folk architecture built about a century ago.

5

6

The new harbour and the settlement of Ayia Ermioni.

Ayia Fotia- Katarraktis - Nenita

Just outside Nehori, left on the main road lies an important monument, directly connected to the island's recent history, the monastery of **Ayios Minas.**

Here in April 1822, 3000 refugees from the city and surrounding villages were killed by the Turks after a desperate resistance. The monastery has since been repaired twice, yet it still carries the scars left by those horrible events.

Back to the main road and down to the left we cross a minor road that leads to **Ayia Fotia**, a lovely pebble beach with quiet turquoise waters. In this serene place there are a few rooms to let and small taverns serving those who love reverie and quiet vacations.

Continuing south the picture changes. On low hills and small valleys we come across eternal olive trees and those small bushes, Chios' famous mastic trees.

Thirteen kms from Hora, is the first mastic village, **Kallimasia**. It used to be one of the island's most important medieval villages, completely encircled by a fortifying wall. Destroyed by the 1881 earthquake, it slowly rises to life ever since.

Ruins of the fortifications and its central tower testify to the vigor the community enjoyed during the Middle Ages and the Genoan occupation. Today the natives are still farming the mastic trees. At the quarters of the Women's Handicraft Association you can admire traditional Chian embroidery.

In Kallimasia you can see the nunnery of **Panagia Plakidiotisa** founded in 1625; the name means

Our Lady of the Tiles after the slates abounding in the area. During Chios' devastation in 1822, over 600 nuns were slaughtered here by the Ottoman army.

The Virgin's lost icon was miraculously found by the only nun who escaped death and later returned to the monastery.

A few kilometers to the east, amidst lush olive groves we come to the coastal community **Katarraktis** (Waterfall).

It is a small, picturesque fishing village with flourishing green gardens, built after the 1881 quakes in the folkloric style of local architecture.

The area is under development, becoming one of the loveliest resorts and still keeping its folklore. The old village Palios (Old) Katarraktis, was built 2 kms southwest in the interior. It is now abandoned, although it attracts the interest of many historians for its ruined medieval houses and byzantine churches.

One of them, **Ayios Ioannis o Argentis** (St. John) is a 14th century domed basilica thoroughly rebuilt except for its vestibule which retains the blind arches, ceramic decoration and the well preserved frescoes. The wooden iconostasis is also of considerable artistic value.

Four kms to the south lies the pictorial village of **Nenita** with a population of 1000 souls. This appellation is derived from the word "neonita" meaning recently - bought refering to farmlands acquired in the 16th century. This is the site of **Panmegiston Taxiarchon** (Great Taxiarchs) monastery, founded i n 1305 commemorating St. Demetrios but renamed a year later after the Taxiarchs. Destroyed by the 1881 earthquakes, it is currently under restoration.

The area's Vokaria coast is the closest point to the Asia Minor shores.

In one kilometer's distance west of Nenita we find **Vouno**, a small village of quaint alleys and tall stone made houses all connected with roof-ways. The "vottes" as these are called were useful when the villagers had to flee from raiders.

Above left: Kallimasia,
Above right: The beach of Agia Fotia.
Below: Katarraktis (Waterfall), a picturesque Chian resort.

Kalamoti - Komi

The village used to have fortifications with castle-gate; from there the view of the surrounding area is majestic.
Leaving Vouno on the way to Patrika, another road to the right will lead you after 3 kms to the villages called Didima. Near **Mesa Didima**, the birthplace of E. Roidis, there is another praise worthy monastery, **Ayia Matrona**. Roidis was planning to build a summer house there but, legend has it, the saint appeared in his sleep and asked him to build a monastery instead. His sisters became the monastery's first two nuns.
During the Turkish occupation, abbot Nikiforos composed his 24 hymns to St. Matrona while staying at the monastery. Today only two or three nuns still live there.
Going south of Didima, passing through Patrika we enter **Kalamoti.**
Long time ago it used to be a large and wealthy mastic village.

Traditional costume from Kalamoti.

Today it numbers less than a thousand residents. In general the village has those characteristics typical to all medieval communities: square design, a fortified wall all around, arches above the streets and well protected narrow alleys between the houses.
Extensive restorations to rehabilitate houses that had collapsed, has altered somewhat its fortress identity. The local dialect is of a great interest as it contains many words from the archaic homeric language. Close to Kalamoti is the temple of **Panayia i Agrelopou**, a chapel with very interesting frescoes. They date back to 14th century and they are rare examples of Paleologian era hagiography. Its gold-leafed, wood-carved iconostasis, an item of 19th c. popular art, blends harmoniously with the rest of the artwork.

The road to Kalamoti sliding towards the south shore, reveals to us the wide plain and beach of Komi.

The soil considered among the island's richest, produces many vegetables and the renown Kalamoti watermelons.

The coast of Komi includes a sand beach, one of Chios' loveliest.

Its blue waters leeward to the north wind, the sea is calm and inviting at all times, ideal for swimming and other marine sports. In recent years **Komi** has been rapidly becoming a modern sea resort.

For the length of the beach there are restaurants serving tempting delicacies, fresh seafood and authentic Greek Cuisine that could fulfill the culinary demands of any visitor.

Between the beach and the stores a tiled walkway offers itself for a stroll at any hour of the day.

On Komi's main street stores are lined up offering wares for the vacationer's everyday

The superb beaches of Chios.
1,2: Komi with its endless sand beach.
3: The pebble beach of Lilika.

needs as well as souvenirs and popular art. Hotels and apartments make your stay comfortable for the summer months.

To the west rises a cone shaped hill with the chapel of Profitis Ilias (Prophet Elias) on its top. From there the view to the prairie and the open sea is just majestic.

The hill's west side faces Emporio and there at its foot some very important ancient ruins have been discovered.

Komi's shore continues to the east reaching **Lilika** another scenic locale.

We return to Kalamoti and take the central road for the city which we catch at Armolia.

6

SOUTHERN CHIOS

Vavili - Schlavia - Armolia- Emporio - Dotia
Pyrgi - Fana - Olimpi - Mesta - Limenas - Vessa

The southern part of Chios presents the traveler with pictures of unique beauty. Rolling hills extend far and wide hugging the sea. They are covered with the green color of mastic trees, these unusual bushes that bear the valuable transparent resin. In the summer the discreet fragrance of mastic is diffused everywhere; timeless olive trees play the counterpoint in this harmonious flora. The roads, most of them in good condition, snaking around the slopes reveal in the last instance the area's little villages. These are the renown Mastic villages, the picturesque village - fortresses with roots in the Middle Ages.

Even though only a few of them survive as in the old, they all retain those characteristics that make them unique. The high walls of the houses in the periphery formed a fortress that protected the mastic - cultivating residents from pillage - minded pirates. There is a central tower and vaulted narrow passageways paved with tiles. When someone wanders through the labyrinthine alleys of Pirgi or Mesta, it is like going centuries back, to a secretive era full of seduction. Today from 27 mastic villages 24 are still intact. Pirgi is a painterly village with traditional motifs scratched on the facade of buildings, a rare and difficult art which survived the passage of centuries. Mesta is one of the best preserved medieval villages and has an external wall, rehabilitated little stone houses and narrow dim lighted alleys. There are also Olympi, Kalamoti, Kallimasia, Nenita, Vessa and Armolia, villages with great byzantine monuments and scattered ruins from the ancient Greek history. A whole ancient town has been unearthed at the cove of Emporio. In Fana you can see the ruins of a famous temple dedicated to Faneos Apollo.

Some of the best beaches can be found in the southern shores of Chios. Mavros Yialos (Black Shore) and adjacent Foki (Seal) both have rounded black lava pebbles, reminders of Psaronas' anger, the area's extinguished volcano.

Picturesque cove in Vroudilia.

Vavili - Armolia

From the city of Chios we get on the central road with a southern course. The road passes through the beautiful mansions of Kampos (Plain) in the interior and leads to the main mastic villages. After the village Vasilioniko, the flatlands and their lush vegetable gardens begin to disappear. Their place is taken now by low hills with sparser vegetation, mainly olive trees. In 8 kms distance from Hora, lies the newer, scenic village of **Vavili**. One km away to the right, a small dirt road leads you amid olive tree groves to the famous church of **Panayia tis Krinas**. Built c. 1287, it is considered an exact replica of Nea Moni. The uneven wall make up has its own charm and the tall cupola blends harmoniously with all the other characteristics. The multitude of the materials and the intense chiaroscuro give an unparalleled vivacity to this sacred space. Its iconostasis has been replaced by a new, wood carved one. On the floor, the original marble navel with a geometric depiction of the five breads is still intact. The decorum of Krina includes works from six different painting periods, marking the evolution of Chian art from the 13th century up to 1734, when the skillful painter Michael Chomatas paints the main church with works characteristic of the Cretan School. At the doorpost a rare illustration symbolizing the vanity of earthy life, deserves special attention.

The same dirt road leads to **Sklavia**, a rural area of immense beauty, water springs with a view to the Kampohoria (villages of the plain) and the eastern shores. Though deserted today, during the Genoan occupation in this area was a big farm with a summer house, possibly property of the Justiniani family. The mass of the buildings, though ruined, is of a great interest to researchers because it is considered the precursor of Kampos' mansions.

The main road splits after Tholopotami (Muddy River). To the left a secondary road takes you to Kalamoti and to the right the main road goes on to Armolia. In this area there is a visible ancient wall 90 m. long and 2 m. high built with huge carved stones. It is known as the Pelasgic Wall, even though its function or the date of its construction remain unknown.

Two kms past the crossroad, right of the way to Kalamoti, on top of a small hill is another important byzantine monument, the chapel of **Panayia Sikelia**, once part of a monastery. The chapel has a unique architectural style, combining elements of a single aisle basilica with a cupola, which ends in a compact cross-like temple. Decorated with ceramics, bricks and walled pots it is a reminder of the capital's byzantine monuments.

South on the main road we arrive at **Armolia**. This community has a very old history, yet most of the old houses have been built anew. The Armolousians have a long tradition in making and decorating ceramics. One of the best iconostasis on the island, carved in 1744 can be found in the church of Panayia, adjacent to the village's central church of Ayios Dimitrios. On a hill west to the village stands the castle of Apolichnon; an inscription still readable says it was built i n 1446 by Ieronymus Justiniani. The castle was elongated, it had its own water reservoirs and interior wooden contructions used as barracks. In some places the castle still retains its original height and bastions. According to historians this was one of several similar fortifications used by the Genovese to protect themselves and police the region.

Leaving Armolia the road on a southwestern course, goes up and down the mastic tree covered hills before it gets to Pirgi. Near there in the Vretou region is the monastery of Zoodohos Pigi (Life - giving Spring). Founded in the 18th c. on the ruins of an old Panayia's church, it became a center of spiritual development for the southerners until it was destroyed in 1822.

Below: Panagia Krina.
Above: The cove of Emporia.

Emporios - Mavros Gialos

Continuing to Pirgi, before the village entrance, to the left of the hospital a snaking road takes you to **Emporio**, 6 kms away.

This picturesque cove has an age long history; already from the Bronze Age, ships traveling through the straits of Chios, could seek shelter from the north winds in its safe harbor; the hill of Profitis Ilias (Prophet Elias) to the east was the main obstacle to the wind. On that hill British archaeologists discovered parts of settlements dating back to the 7th or 8th century B.C.

On the southern slope parts of an ancient citadel's wall were found along with a right angled, flat roofed temple of the 6th century B.C. believed to be dedicated to goddess Athena. Below the citadel one - room houses formed a thick habitational maze.

The area seems to have been abandoned peacefully by the end of the ancient era.

It is believed to be Leukonion mentioned by historian Thoucidides.

At the cove's temple several historical
periods from 690 B.C. to the Paleochristian
era can be distinguished.
Here the remnants of a well crafted Ionian -
style temple were also found.
To the left of the harbor rises the presently
extinguished volcano Psaronas that once
covered with lava everything around it.
That explains the existence of the pitch -
black pebbles found in the two beaches
nearby, namely **Mavros Gialos** and **Foki**.

*A high view of Emporio,
one of Chio's idyllic coves.*

These pebbles were used to pave the yards
of the Kampos' mansions and many houses
in Hora. Emporio's beaches are of
astonishing beauty; the sea darkened
by the reflection of the black pebbles, offers
cordially its freshness to those seeking it.
A nicely paved path, a sign that people care,
connects the two beaches. Today's Emporio
is consisted principally of summer houses.
It has to offer apartments and pensions to let,
as well as restaurants and shops operating
for the summer period. Despite the intrusion
of modernity, the small harbor remains calm
and idyllic.

Dotia - Vroulidia

Going a bit back, to the main road that leads
to Pirgi we come to a junction with the road to
Thotia, a region formerly known as a hunting
area. Thotia is the largest mastic field of Pirgi.
Archaeological digs have discovered a
prehistoric habitation and tombs carved on
stone. Pottery from these tombs is exhibited
at the Archaeological Museum of Chios.
Thotia is dominated by a well preserved
Genoan tower. The structure is three leveled,
domed, with bastions and big openings
upstairs. It used to be surrounded by small
turrets, one on each corner; now only one
of them is barely discernible.
Continuing south the road ends in a plateau
of the Vroulidia area, 50 m. above sea level.
The view from there is stunning as the blue
of the sky blends in the distance with the blue
of the archipelago. From there a long staircase
coils down to the cool bosom of the sea.
To go back we take Emporio's road upwards
and left towards Pirgi.

The three beaches with the unique volcanic pebbles (from the left): Foli, Mavros Yialos, Emboreio.

Pirgi, "the painterly village"

It is the largest and for many the most important of the medieval villages.

The community of Pirgi attracts great interest for its city plan and architectural design.

Despite the changes inflicted upon it by time and human interference, Pirgi even in our days, is a living legend coming deep from the Middle Ages. The structure of its fortifications attributed histori- cally to the Genovese, is the application of Greek city planning developed in various medieval monasteries (Mt. Athos, Daphne, Osios Meletios to ward off enemy raids.

Today, one can discern traces of the perimeter's stone wall with four corner turrets that once pro- tected the village.

Originally the village was a four-sided enclosure with a thick habitational web.

The houses in the periphery were all built in absolutely unbroken contact with no doors or windows on the outside, thus forming an unas- sailable wall.

People entered the village through two heavy iron gates, the Low Entrance (Kato Porta) in the middle of the eastern wall and the High Entrance (Pano Porta) in the west side. The gates were shut during nighttime and naturally for defensive purposes. In the corners of the four sided wall turrets were used as observatories. Similar defensive role played the watches placed in key positions from shore to village.

The watchmen were in visual contact and in the case of danger the message was transmitted all the way to the village and to those working in the fields, by a series of fires.

The extensive defense plans taken by the local lords and the villagers, besides telling something about the architectural economy of the area, is a strong indicator of the area's wealth and the pirates perninicious attemps to put a hand on it.

Pirgi, the largest medieval village.

Ayioi Apostoli (saints Apostles) appear through the darkness.

From the village's center, proud and despotic rose the Tower, the building after which the largest of the mastic villages was named.

A defensive as well as an administrative center, the tower was built by the Genoans at the core of the settlement near the central square.

The massive rectangular stone building was in the middle of a thick wall and had a small turret on each corner.

There were no openings at ground level; Entrance was made possible by mobile elements fitted to the outside wall, or by ladders that were subsequently pulled upstairs. Thus in case of enemy attack, the tower could be isolated fast and easily, protecting the residents' lives and making things hard for the raiders.

From an architect's point of view, the tower was a three story structure, ground floor and two levels, with six notched bastions on each side of the top level and six arched windows on each side of the middle floor, reaching a total height of 18 m. Unfortunately today only parts of the tower survive.

It was during the Turkish occupation that the tower was totally abandoned, while the 1881 quake destroyed its east and west sides beyond repair. In 1937 the town hall decided to demolish 3 m. from the upper level, fearing it would fall.

Inside the tower there are still a few houses, built originally in 1892, which partly contributed to the tower's preservation. Time though was more graceful with Pirgi's other historical monuments.

Ayioi Apostoli (Saints Apostles) the church in the end of the domed corridor beginning from the central square, is a finely preserved byzantine monument. Although its foundation is placed between the 13th and 14th centuries, both its exterior elements (cupolas, blind arches, door posts, round pediments) and the frescoes decorating the interior walls - painted by Domestihos Kinigos of Crete, are still in excellent condition.

A few meters away from this priceless gem, in the central square rises commandingly the church of Kimisis Tis Theotokou (Our Lady's Dormition). Built in 1694 the three aisled basilica which hosts on the ground floor of its belfry the chapel of Ayios Antonios (St. Anthony), today it still functions as the village's main Church.

It is worthy visiting the community's other two religious monuments; the church of Taxiarches (1680) in the south and the even older church of Ipapanti in the northwest border of the village.

There is also the monastery of **Ayios Georgios** (St. George, 19th c.), its guest house decorated with the "Ksista", the famous patterns scratched on the facades of buildings.

The general rule underlying the houses here is saving space. The houses, tight spaced, built to height rather than width and next to each other, are forming opposing rows separated by narrow alleys.

Often these alleys are connected with half cylindrical domes, creating the "skepasta", that being arcades and bows, which besides making extra ground rooms, more importantly, they facilitated the residents' monement above ground.

In other instances above the streets, buttresses supporting these domes on both sides are forming small bridges.

All of the old houses principally two storied and made of stone to repel arson and fires, have similar interior structures.

The ground level tight and dim lighted, was used as storage and stables.

One can get to the rooms by an interior staircase which also leads to the "clear", the open space inside the first level, a source of air and sunlight and which had access to the dome by a stairway. The houses' rooms were all about the same height and were connected by bows or arcades so that they formed aerial walkways from which the residents could move to any place in the village they pleased.

Undoubtedly the principal characteristic of these houses is the scratched patterns decorating their facades. Theories on the origin of this impressive art are divided.

Some maintain that it is the descendant of a parallel "graffiti" art from Genoa.

Others believe it originated in Byzantium, specifically in Constantinople. Whatever its origins the Pirgians loved and developed this form of exterior decorating, keeping it alive to our days.

Going back in time one can distinguish three different periods of the "ksista" (scratches).

An early period that stretches up to the second half of the 19th c. and includes a limited number of patterns usually rectangles or rhombuses repeated to cover the whole facade.

Ksista of that period can be found almost everywhere in Chios.

The second period, from the beginning of this century until about 1950 carries the mark of master Georgios Kountouris or Vatte who specialized in this technique in Constantinople.

The themes of this period include new embellished geometric forms and free depictions of flora and fauna.

In the same period there is wide spread use of the "circle with its moons", done in a great color variety.

The third period in which we are now is characterized by changes in the materials, reduction of color and limited creative activity.

Today there are groups of artisans and workers who specialize in this craft.

The process is relatively simple though it requires experience and knowledge.

The artisans, on the surface to be decorated, first they spread a mixture of sand, asbestos and cement and then cover it with white asbestos.

Then they draw carefully the various patterns in strictly horizontal zones and finally they scratch lightly with a kitchen fork the appropriate parts of the surface asbestos to reveal the underlying darker substratum.

The scratched motifs named after this last phase of the process, depending on what they depict are given special names such as mill's wing, flag, chalice, moons etc.

In Pirgi one can enjoy highly artistic and aesthetic compositions such as the ones on Taxiarches chapel or the house of Tsikis, attributed to the great master G. Kountouris.

Unique, unforgettable scenes from Pyrgi, full of color and tradition.

His two talented sons Nikolaos and Constantinos followed on his steps successfully and in 1934 were funded by Phillipos Argentis to decorate a number of the main square's buildings, giving it a homogeneous look.

Walking the idyllic narrow alleys of Pirgi, the visitor seems to be going back to the Middle Ages. In the summer the smell of mastic is spread everywhere. From the little balconies-recent additions to the houses, hanging tomatine pots enrich with their bright reds the gray stones with the characteristic scratched motifs.

Leaving the village the visitor takes with him-her these rare impressions to cherish forever.

Approximately one and a half km. Distance from Pirgi on the road to Olympi and Mesta, heaps of stones inside an olive grove indicate the presence of an old settlement. It is Managros a small village abandoned by its residents who moved to Pirgi during the Genoan occupation.

Here survive the ruins of two small Christian churches; marble parts from Ionian style columns of the classical antiquity have been also found here and can be seen in the Archaeological Museum of Chios.

At the north end of the road, in the region of historical Keros another medieval settlement containing ruins of churches built with ancient materials.

Pirgi's central square
and church of Theotokos.

Fana - Olympi

Just outside Pirgi on the way to Olympi,
a road to the left takes you south to the cove
of **Fana** once used by ancient navigators
as safe anchorage. Fana is an ancient name
deriving from Faneos Apollon. The road passes
through a valley of olive tree groves and ends
in a beautiful deserted sand beach offered
for swimming. The ancient temple's ruins lie
on top of a hill near the shore and date back
to the 6th c. BC. The temple was built in Ionian
style with island marble and local limestone.
Findings from this temple are kept in the
Archaeological Museum of Chios. Strabo
refers to this temple, saying it was located
in the middle of a palm tree grove.
In the antiquity the famous "wine from Fana"
was also produced here.
We return on the main road and not far from
there we encounter **Olympi**, another important
medieval village with the appearance of a fort.
The unity of the houses' walls in the periphery
is eminent. They had not openings for windows
and obviously functioned as fortifications.
There is also a central gate, a defensive tower in
the center of the village and narrow labyrinthine
streets with vaults and stone bows connecting
the houses. Current house renovations have
altered the village's character.
The tower is still standing there but half ruined.
There is a chapel in the square, that of **Ayia
Paraskevi** (St. Friday); Its wood carved
iconostasis is an important example of 18th
century art. From the Middle Ages comes
the "Trapeza" (Dining Room) of Olympi situated
at Vlihos and still in good condition.
It is a two story building consisted of an
elongated chamber on each floor.
Each room contains stone built benches
and tables used for centuries to facilitate
the traditional wedding meals of Olympi
marriages. From Olympi we continue west
towards Mesta.

Impressive memories from Olympi.

The Cave of Olympi

This is in the area of Sykia in Olympi.
This cave has an exceptionally rich stalactite
adornment, making it one of the finest
and most beautiful caves of Greece,
despite its small dimensions (40 m in
diameter with a height of 2-10 m).
It is considered one of the most remarkable
caves in the Balkans, with the largest
number of stalactites and stalagmites per
square metre. Its artificial entrance is at an
altitude of 110 m above sea level. The cave
is still active, meaning that the processes
by which the stalactites are formed are still
continuing. For this reason much care is
needed so as not to disturb the balance
within its internal microclimate.
Studies show that the cave was formed
in two phases. The first was during the
Mesozoic period (150 million years ago)
and the second in the Cenozoic period
(65 million years ago).
The stalactites (hanging from the roof
of the cave) and the stalagmites
(rising from the floor) are formed of
calcium salts deposited by dripping water
that has permeated through the limestone.
In certain spots the adornment of the cave
has a white colour. As a rule, however, it
has more of a yellow-red hue due to the
admixture of aluminium elements.
The cave also features some very
impressive and rare unusual stalactite
complexes, formed by stalactites that are
not growing in a directly downward direction
and thus contravening the law of gravity.
The cave was initially a blind precipice
without any opening and with no trace of
human presence. At some point a large
rock became detached from the roof
and created a natural opening.
The sunlight which beams in through
the roof at certain hours of the day
creates a visually unique experience
when absolute darkness prevails
in the cave.

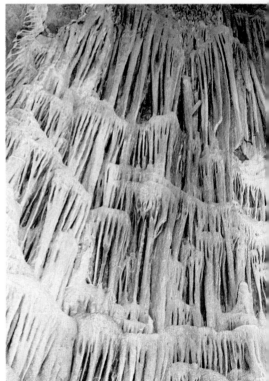

Mesta

Mesta is the best preserved mastic village. It has the most sights to see and a large tourist turnaround.

It is also one of the prettiest fort-villages bustling with life and proud of its history.

Arriving at the perimeter wall of a tower with 3 guardian turrets in its corners, the visitor begins his or hers personal tour of the Middle Ages.

The community built in the byzantine years, had in the 12th c. its fortifications improved by the Genoans.

Behind the central gate, the so called "captain's door", two of the villages oldest churches Ayios Georgios (St. George) and Ayia Paraskevi (St. Friday) containing excellent frescoes, introduce us to a deeply religious world.

As we walk we come across many churches the oldest of which is Old Taxiarch, from 1412 and for many centuries the village's main church. Today this role belongs to the church of Taxiarchon, one of the largest on Chios, founded in 1868 at the site of the round central tower.

The main square "the prairie" as the locals call it, is the only open space in this whole fort-village.

Here the villagers congregated for all social purposes, celebrations, marriages and fairs. Today the square still has that beautiful old color, bustling with life especially in the summer months.

There are taverns offering good food, coffee shops and a small bar; all serve an indigenous wine which is among Chios' best.

Another local product is "souma is a kind of ouzo made by distilling figs. A beverage for heavy drinkers souma is pure and uniquely tasting, produced exclusively in this area.

Mesta, the best preserved village-fort.

Wandering through the maze of Mesta's narrow, vaulted alleys the visitor discovers infinite big and small legends telling just by their presence the village's long history. One of these legends is Milita's tower situated northwest; it has played a decisive role in defending Mesta against pirate raids. The houses tightly packed next to each other, small and tidy, built like miniature fortresses have the same architectural elements we encounter in all medieval villages. What most impresses the visitor though, is that Mesta has kept most of its characteristics unchanged; and as these reminders of the old romantic era blend with the intoxicating scent of the mastic, they cause an exquisite feeling to the modern traveler, a feeling never to be forgotten.

Yet the value of this superb mastic village does not lie only in its archaeological meaning; Mesta above all is a vivacious, hospitable place with powerful tradition incarnated in its various cultural manifestations.

At the same time Mesta is a good starting point for the lovers of natural beauty, since all around it are situated Trahilia, Avlonia, Merikounda, Limenas, and Didima, some of the best beaches in Chios.

The church of the Taxiarch,
with its ornate carved wooden iconostasis
is surrounded by covered alleyways of unique beauty.

Vessa, another beautiful mastic village.

Limenas-Mesta

Leaving Mesta, as the road winds to the north amid bushy hills, **Mesta's seaport Limenas** appears suddenly in front of us, about 40 km. away from the city of Chios.

The deep enclosed bay is a natural leeward port, suitable even for larger ships.

Strabo called it "Notion" which meant Southern.

Lately Limenas the small fishing village has been developing very rapidly.

It already has a hotel, restaurants and taverns serving fresh fish and seafood specialties.

After Limenas the road continues northbound following the shore.

The landscape becomes rough, the vegetation rich and the coast forms bays and isolated coves suitable for swimming and fishing.

Along this way we encounter Didima (Twins), Kato Elata (Low Firs), and Ayia Irini (St. Irene) which has a chapel and a lonely fish tavern right on the coast.

Fried smellts and marinated octopus are some of the dishes the travellers enjoy here.

Vessa - Ayios Georgios

On the way back we pass through the medieval villages Elata (Firs) and Vessa. Vessa once a fort - village, today though pretty, retains very little from that old character.

Onwards to the east about 8 km. away, is the village of **Ayios Georgios** (St. George) **Sikousis**. Built on the top of a wooded hill 400 m. above the sea, it has a majestic view of Kampos, the Aegean sea and the Asia minor coast. The community was founded in 1518 by the monk Sofronios Sepsis who organized the first peasants around an abandoned monastery of St. George. Its church is believed to be a faithful replica of Nea Moni and though it has suffered many renovations, it still has the aura of the past. The road goes through Zifia, birthplace of byzantine history professor and member of the Academy, mr Amantos, continues to Halkio (Copper owing its name to the copper tone of its soil and through Kampos (Plain), it ends in the middle of Hora.

One of Vessa's beautiful alleys.

7

CENTRAL CHIOS

Karies - Ayios Markos - Nea Moni - Ayioi Pateres
Avgonima - Anavatos - Lithi

The tour of central Chios can be one of the most impressive itineraries of the island. The road cuts through a solitary, rough, mountainous landscape with thick vegetation and sparse villages to conclude downward in the serene and beautiful west shores from where the sunsets are immaculate. The ascent on the central range of Provation Mountain (Mt. Sheep) that rises up to a thousand m., offers an excellent view of Chios and of the Asia Minor coast opposite. On the way we come upon Nea Moni (New Abbey), the imposing monastery that stands here for ten centuries, guarding Orthodoxy and Hellenism, capturing the imagination of every visitor. Even the most unsuspecting becomes impressed by the church of Theotokos (Mother of God) and its huge cupola; from the windows high up, the light bathes the sacred space exciting the emotions and inspiring awe for the Holly Greatness. This itinerary includes more interesting monasteries and churches such as Panayia Kourna, Saint Mark's cloister and Ayion Pateron Abbey.

Next the road takes us through a thick pine forest to Avgonima, a 11th c. little village built on a plateau with an excellent view to the west shores. A little further to the north clambered on the steep rocks and hard to be seen lies Anavatos the Aegean's Mystras, the village that has no rival. Unassailable from any direction this medieval village - fort with the abandoned stone houses and a citadel on the edge of the abyss, is a living ghost town adding more greatness to this wild landscape. A historical place, Anavatos was besieged stubbornly before it fell heroically to the avenging soldiers. Leaving from Anavatos, we descend westwards where nature now becomes more friendly. The shore road passes by Elinda bay an ancient harbor and then turning south, heads for Lithi a coastal community with a superb view to the sea. In Lithi' bay there is a long sand beach, one of Chios' best. There on the beach's taverns the visitor can enjoy a variety of rare fresh fish and tasty tidbits from the traditional Greek cuisine.

Karies - Ayios Markos

From the town of Chios (Hora) starts a road traversing central Chios as it ascends to Nea Moni. Outside the city we first see the new nunnery of Panayia (Our Lady). Six km. further, is the beautiful village of **Karies** (chestnut trees); it has cool climate, fresh springs and a majestic view of the city, Kampos, the open sea and the Asia Minor coast.

Next is the small monastery of **Panayia Kourna**, possibly the Dominican abbey of Theotokos Incoronata (Crowned Mother of God) in the Genoan era.

Now the road climbs even higher on the main range of the Provation Mount where a lush pine forest begins; not far from the left side of the road is the **cloister of Ayios Markos** (St. Mark), accessible but not without some difficulty. It dates from 1700 but its buildings belong to a later period. Up there the view is really dream like.

Nea Moni

About half way between east and west, 15 km. from Hora stands Nea Moni (New Monastery). Its compound with the large church, the buildings and the tall cypresses is awe inspiring as it rises alone in the middle of the mountainous landscape. It is the most important christian and historical monument on the whole island. According to tradition, 3 Chian hermits, Nikitas, Ioannis and Iosef discovered the miracle working icon of Theotokos hanging from the boughs of a myrtle tree located at the site of today's sanctuary. The icon survived to our days in a miraculous way. The three hermits were befriended by Constantinos o Monomahos (the Combatant) then in exile in neighboring Lesvos. He promised them to build a church where the icon was found if he was soon to become an emperor.

View of Nea Moni.

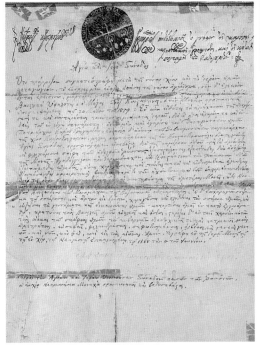

Golden bull for Nea Moni.

Part of Nea Moni.

Indeed in two years, Monomahos unexpectedly became the Emperor of Byzantium and respectfully fulfilled his promise.

Top architects were sent from Constantinople to build Nea Moni.

The works lasted for 12 years; after the emperor's death, they were continued by empress Theodora, who sould no less real than her predecesson in building Nea Moni.

The architecture of Nea Moni's church is a good example of the elegant octagonal style encountered only in Chios and Cyprus.

The church's central area is a square with a cupola that has no supports, making the interior a continuous free space that overwhelms the faithful. The cupola is proportionally huge and especially high (15.5 m.) with corresponding windows that illuminate the interior with abundant light.

The whole support system is considered very daring, a high point of architecture, linking N. Moni to similar monuments in Constantinople. All the interior walls underneath the mosaic zone were covered by elaborate fake marble panels.

Small ornamental columns in the corners, decorated all eight piers supporting the arches.

At the entrances the door frames were made of marble.

The floors were covered with colorful marble cut in panels that had round emblems.

The iconostasis was made of pure white marble as is the new one today.

On it you can see the historic, miracle working icon of Theotokos which was found on site.

The original cupola had interior undulations and its exterior was covered with lead - sheets.

The narthex was dim lighted compared to the nave.

The porch has suffered subsequent renovations yet retains the grace and old grandeur coming from three domes and the side cylindrical concavities all combined to a cross.

The exterior walls are covered with white plaster.

Despite all the changes, today the characteristics reminiscent of the byzantine capital's architecture are still discernible.

Only parts of the mosaics survive today, enough though for the visitor to appreciate their art.

The emperor Constantine Monomahos made sure he provided with the best artists 11th century Constantinople could supply.

The art works are characterized by vivacity and originality of style. The mosaics covered the nave and porch surface from the hight of the arches and up. Their excellent technique is evident by the homogeneity of the decorum, even in the more difficult curved surfaces of the interior.

The mosaic's themes were adapted to the byzantine decorative dogma of the period.

The Pantocrator of the original cupola was surrounded by full blown angels in a gold - leafed backround that covered all undulations.In the spherical triangles below the four Evangelists were depicted along with four Cherubims.

From that only a small part still survives. In the eight concavities below, the cycle of Christ's life was illustrated. In the three hollows of the sanctuary were a praying Child-less Theotokos and the Archangels Michael and Gabriel. In the narthex besides the Virgin and saint Anna there is a zone of male saints. In the small central cupola, around the Virgin were lined eight military angels.

Despite the austerity of the portrayals, the details and characteristics of saints show the wealth of the compositions and the unique character of byzantine art.

Dominant and intense blues, greens and dark reds blend harmoniously with the gold leaves playfully reflecting the light.

That makes the expressivity of the faces even more intense. The sense of the three - dimensional is canceled by the colors and the deep, strict look on the faces becomes more austere by the intense shadowing underneath the eyes, marking the highly religious character of the temple. Only a few of the church's artifacts survive today, among which is a gold - threaded altar cover, the renown "Pefki" (Pine), the sole example of the excellent 17th c. Chian knitting art.

From the rest of N. Moni's buildings, the water reservoir survives from the 11th c. still unblemished, made wholly of white marble.

It is a large single space covered by 16 spherical blind domes that are supported by 8 marble columns.

The east side of the cistern is arched, ornamented by ceramic arcades. Southwest of the church is the location of the "Trapeza" (dining room); there the long dining table is coated with colored marble.

The tower in the monastery's west border built by the Genoans, protected the monks during those dreaded pirate raids. Its attic had horizontal cornices above the small arches supporting the roof.

In the chapel of the Holly Cross (Timios Stavros), a late addition to the compound, the bones of those massacred in 1822 are kept until today. The monk's cells in the west wing have been turned into a small museum, where important relics from the monastery's long history are exhibited.

With the passing of centuries the abbey suffered many evils, from the 13th c. Saracen raiders to the Turks who in 1822 pillaged everything in sight and massacred all the Chians who had sought refuge there.

The Turks returned 1828 to inflict more destruction; to conclude the catastrophe came the 1881 earthquakes which all but deserted the monastery.

Nea Moni is today under restoration, slowly regaining its old byzantine grandeur. Administratively the abbey was under the direct jurisdiction of the Patriarch in Constantinople. During the Turkish occupation, for a long period it enjoyed autonomy. Every August 23rd when the Virgin's Dormition is commemorated, a large number of pilgrims flocks to the monastery.

The decoration of the main church of Nea Moni is very impressive with the Pantocrator in the dome in addition to its sumptuous mosaics.

Ayioi Pateres - Avgonima

Leaving N. Moni with a westward direction, in close distance lies the chapel of **Agion Pateron** (Holly Fathers) founded by monk Pahomios to commemorate the three hermits who found the miraculous icon of Theotokos and established Nea Moni.

This western course on the main road is of unique beauty. The thick pine forest lasts all the way down to Avgonima.

The 11th c. village is situated on a plateau, its architecture typically medieval with tall stone houses, small windows and narrow alleys.

From **Avgonima** the view of the west shores and the sunset is very impressive. Here one can stay overnight in beautiful medieval houses with modern accommodations. Four km. away to the north lies Anavatos. The traveler must first get very close to clearly make out the houses nested upon the rugged rocks. One must really know the village is there in order to see it.

Anavatos

The sight of **Anavatos** is deeply impressive and awe inspiring.

A whole village perched on top of a granite rock at the end of a cliff. The only way to reach it is from the south.

The road snakes upwards from the foot of the rock to the village's entrance.

All around deep, unspoiled, shadowy ravines complement the landscape.

Even its name Anavatos (inaccessible) reveals the reason it was built there.

Its strategic natural location and the wall protected the villagers from the pirates raiding the west coast.

It is said that the village was originally built on a nearby site by byzantine lumberjacks brought to build Nea Moni, by emperor Constantine the Combatant.

Yet the residents for reason of the frequent raids, never took root there.

Avgonima, a solitary medieval village.

Thus Anavatos ended in this inaccessible but well protected area. This may be the reason many believe the existing village is posterior to the rest of the medieval villages in the south.

The villagers grew olive trees, pistachio trees and cultivated the vine in the fertile land that extends all the way to Avgonima.

At the end of the 18th c., refugees from Ionia brought with them the knowledge of tobacco cultivation. Anavatos reached its apogee in the last years of the Turkish occupation. Nevertheless the village did not escape the Turk's wrath in 1822, nor the power of the 1881 quakes which also left indelible marks.

The settlement stretches in the form of an amphitheater from the rock's lowest points up to the citadel and the cliff.

The houses about 400 in number, are two leveled and rectangular. Instead of roof there is a horizontal wooden attic and it is all built with stones held together by a gray clay.

They are built tightly next to each other with low doors, arched windows and skylights functioning as observatories, showing how carefully they had been planned , to offer the maximum possible security.

In the village's south where the only access was, the height of fortifications was 2m. and long ago there had been an iron gate.

Near the gate there used to be a three story building about 15m. tall. On its ground floor was housed the olive oil mill; today the oil-press' two huge round slabs are still there.

On the second floor there was the school and on the third the church of Theotokos and the precious water reservoir.

Up on the citadel, two aisled and double roofed was built the church of the Taxiarch. Today only its uniquely arcaded walls still survive.

A picture of the Archangel has been moved to entrance of the new church of Taxiarchis where more relics from the village's old churches are now kept.

Most of the buildings are well preserved and as a whole they put forth an image of a living ghost town, adding to the sublimity of this rough country.

Icons from the village and the people of Anavatos.

That is why many call Anavatos "the Aegean's Mystras".

The village has been deemed a national monument to be preserved under the law and restoration works have already begun.

Around the first turn outside Anavatos is the chapel of Ai Yiorgis (St. George).

Surviving in good condition since the 16th century, it has a good part of its frescoes still intact.

This single - aisled basilica is all built with Chian stone. Its iconostasis is newer and with no special value.

Across the chapel is a memorial for those fallen in the 1822 battle against the Turks.

Elinda - Lithi

Going back to Avgonima a road takes us west
to the shore road and from there to Elinda bay,
right below Anavatos.

Elinda is a deep bay with a pebble beach
and Strabo says, in the ancient times it was
used as a port. In its bottom rests a Roman
shipwreck, marking the Romans' attempt
to link Chios via its west coast,
to the Hellenic mainland.

Following the shore road towards the
southwest we pass by **Lithi,** a village
overlooking the coast, full of green and a
majestic view of the open sea.

A road to the right takes you to Lithi's beach,
a long sand beach stretching in front of an
open Lithi bay. The sea with its calm blue
waters invites the traveler to enjoy its coolness,
while several outdoor taverns serve a great
variety of fresh exotic fish, seafood and many
tempting traditional Greek delicacies.

As in all the west shores of Chios,
it is worth staying here to experience the
fantastic sunset. To return to the city,
one heads south to Vessa and then east
via Ayios Georgios Sikousis.

Across: Lithi, stone vaulted alley.
Below: Elinda's cove.

8

NORTH - EAST CHIOS

Vrontados - Daskalopetra - Sikiada - Lagatha
Kardamila - Nagos - Fita - Pitios

Chios' eastern shores show an intense fragmentation forming countless bays and coves. Following the coast, initially we pass by Vrontados, Chios' pretty suburb with the well made houses and the lavish gardens. Here is where operate the fully organized beaches of Chios, suitable for marine sports. The road passes through the historic site of Daskalopetra, the teaching post of Homer, from then on the landscape becomes rocky and the coast precipitous. The monastery of Mitsinidi to the right, literally leans over the waves. Next the rocks give way to sparse vegetation. On the way to the north we encounter picturesque fishing villages with nice beaches and hospitable taverns: Lagatha, the historic Kardamila - an old medieval village with lots of sightseeing. In Kardamila bay, the coastal community Marmaro (Marble) is becoming a resort while keeping its traditions. To the north of Marmaro is Nagos a small oasis with running spring waters and thick vegetation; it comes all the way to a tiny pebble beach that has fish taverns right on the waves. The road goes uphill and the scenery becomes rough. The northern hinterland with its few, poor, little villages presents us with a different picture of multifaceted Chios. The road climbs up passing the communities of Armades, Viki and Kampia. In an isolated area we come upon the monastery of Moundon, also known as the monastery of Prodromos (John the Baptist); it was abandoned from the byzantine years, but it still possesses excellent frescoes. On the reverse direction, going back to the town of Chios, a detour from the main road of Hora - Volissos, leads to Pitios village, the only one in northern Chios with a medieval character. The last impression from this itinerary is the majestic view of the eastern shores extending before our eyes.

Vrontados

Commencing from Hora, the northbound road runs almost on the same course with the coastline. Just passed the area Livadia (Prairies) you can see the ruins of the **Ayios Isidoros** (St. Isidore) basilica. Saint Isidore was born in Alexandria and became a martyr in Chios during the reign of Dekius (250 A.D.) Saint Isidore is the patron saint of the island and many churches are dedicated to his memory. The church was built in the 5th c. and has undergone extensive repairs since. The Saint's relics as well as those of St. Merope were kept here until they were taken away by the Venetians. Going north, 5 km. from the city is the suburb of **Vrontados**, today just an extension of the expanding city. The community is relatively recent and includes a greater area where most of the houses are owned by people employed in the merchant marine. In their majority the houses are well built with vegetable and flower gardens in between. Vrontados' symbol is the "Unknown Sailor" memorial, the work of the well known Chian sculptor Thanassis Apartis. It is located on the shore road, across the Town Hall. In Upper Vrontados is the Museum of the Friends of Progress Club, where artifacts of the Chian marine tradition such as ship replicas, wood carvings and old relics are exhibited.

In Vrontados' Lo bay operates one of Chios' best beaches, organized with modern accommodations for the bathers, marine sports and a luxurious restaurant. The beach boasts for its Blue Flag, an honorary sign given by the European Union. Here is also the monastery of Ayios Stefanos (St. Stephan) founded in 1880. Saint Parthenios took the monastery under his protection and rebuilt the church. His memory is celebrated on December 27th.

Vrontados, the beautiful coastal suburb of Chios.

Daskalopetra - Sikiada

Next is another beautiful beach, Daskalopetra (Teacher's Rock) also known as Pasha's fountain. The area is at the foot of Mount Epos, rich in vegetation and watersprings. Legend has it that blind Homer was left here by sailors of a ship coming from the Erithrea coast opposite. Just above there is **Daskalopetra**, or Daskalio, or Homer's Rock.

It is a large rock, chiseled flat on its upper surface, where Homer stood, the legend goes, to teach his students. On the rock's southwest side is a cubic altar with worn out reliefs, 1 m. high and made of that same rock. It is believed to be an archaic plain air sanctuary of goddess Cybele worshipped by the Phrygians living across the straits.

Leaving Daskalopetra the road ascends, as the shores become rugged. On a plateau not too far to the right, is the marble tomb of philologist and author Yiannis Psycharis who died in 1929. On the column his verses and inscriptions can be read. From this plateau the visitor can enjoy the excellent view of surrounding scenery, Vrontados and the Asia Minor coast opposite.

As the road continues northbound, we get to the cloister of Mirsinidio also known as **Panayia i Mirtidiotisa** (Our Lady of the Myrtles). Built on the edge of an inclining slope, it almost leans over the waves.

It has a history of 100 years and in its vestry can be found relics and other sacred artifacts of Chian history. The landscape takes on a wild beauty, as the road comes dangerously close to the cliffs. We pass the cove of Miliga and that

of Agios Ioannis tou Tholou (St. John of the Cupola) which has a small craft dockyard. Next on line is the bay and community of **Pantoukios**. Overlooking Pantoukios is **Sikiada** (Fig Trees), a sailor's community with new and old houses. The name of the village was earned from the fig trees once abundant in the area.

On the road to the next village we see Koidianta, an abandoned community. During the German occupation it was a stronghold of the greek Resistance. Today a memorial reminds the young of these heroic Chians.

Daskalopetra, the site where, according to tradition Homer taught.

Lagada

In three km. comes to sight the little port of
Lagadas (Ravine), built in the middle of a wide,
fertile gorge. Boats to Inouses depart
frequently from here. The area abounds with
vegetable gardens, olive and fruit trees and
there are some wind mills in the area.
The houses are built plain with ceramic roofs.
Over Lagada we can barely see Agrelopos.
The next cove up is ancient Delfini (Dolphin),
its mouth obstructed by the islet Tavros (Bull)
in the location Givari - a Latin derived word,
meaning fishery (vivarium). Delfini had all the
requirements of a naval base.
According to historian Thoucidides,
the Athenians stormed Delfini and fortified it,
in their attempt to keep an alliance with the
Ionian cities and Chios, an ally of Sparta since
411 B.C. It took the Spartans five whole years
to recapture Delfini.

Above: The picturesque cove of Lagada.
Below: Aerial picture of Pantoukios.

Kardamila

The road now continues to **Kardamila**, an ancient Chian community with centuries of uninterrupted life. Ano Kardamila left on the slope where it has always been and Kato Kardamila or Marmaro (Marble) is the newer, pretty settlement built in the recess of Marmaro Bay. Further on the same shore is Rahi, another new settlement of Kardamila. The denizens of this area used to be peasants and herders who later turned to the sea. The region is proud for its renown seamen, ship-owners too. Unfortunately, in Kardamila only few artifacts of this long history survive.

Just before the entrance to Ano Kardamila rises the hill of Gria (Old Woman) with ruins of medieval fortifications from three round towers; the precipitous cliff complements the defensive line. There are also marks from an old Hellenistic wall.

During the Middle Ages and the Ottoman era, the village was one of Chios' largest. It played an important role in the Independence War of 1821. It is said, this was the only village never captured by the Turks. The architecture is plain here too; old and new houses with ceramic roofs add their difference to the scenery.

The Kardamila Friends of Progress Club founded in 1979, has raised considerably the cultural level of the village. Important artistic and cultural events are being organized attracting everybody's interest. Kato Kardamila is progressing touristically, offering the visitor comfortable stay and beautiful old houses for quiet vacations. The fish taverns of the area offer rare seafood delicacies and fresh fish.

Kardamila bay and the village.

There is some more sightseeing to be done in Kardamila's area, such as the old settlement of Spilies (Caves), the churches of **Ayios Nikolaos** St. Nickolas) **Prinaritis** and **Ayios Georgios** (St. George), the latter with 16th c. frescoes and a pretty belfry, Kimisis tis Theotokou (Dormition of Mary) - built in the ruins of the older **Pera Panayia**, the statue of "the Captain" carved by Thanassis Apartis, and the picturesque windmill in Mavri Agali (Black Bosom).

Nagos - Viki - Fita

Six km. to the north, the road comes to the region of Nagos, a small oasis with running watersprings and lush vegetation terminated in the **bay of Nagos**, endowed with a toy - like pebble beach. The name Nagos comes from the word "naos" (temple) and indeed an ancient temple was unearthed here during the excavations of 1921.

Kardamila Cove.

Later a church of Panagia was built on the same site. The small bay of Nagos has been distinguished with the Blue Flag of the European Union.
Here on the cliffs overlooking the sea two small hotel units and a couple of taverns await the visitors.
Further north, good for swimming is the beautiful beach of Yosona or Iasona (Jason) as it was known in the ancient times. Here too, originating in the Pelineo Mountains, run watersprings making the land especially fertile. The road continues uphill, steep as it climbs away from the shore towards the north. The northern villages we see on the way have very little in common with those of the south, as they blend with the rough and rugged mountainous terrain. They consist of small, simple, unornamented houses owned by peasants and herders, all built in a loose order. For the roofs, instead of built domes, processed lumber is used. First one in our itinerary is the **Amades** village, where one of the oldest wood carved iconostasis survives. Three km. away follows **Viki** with just a few residents.
Here visible are the traces of a triangular medieval wall with three turrets and a defensive tower in the middle.
In 6km. we come upon Kampia the smallest mountainous village. Those three villages are famous for their good - tasting cherries.
From there the road literally climbs up to the highest point of Chios, reaching an elevation of 1297 m. The next village is **Fita** with a defensive tower standing there since 1516. The landscape is now clearly mountainous, completely different from the rest of Chios.
After **Kipouries**, in a desolate region we find **Moni Moundon**,
an abandoned monastery dedicated to John the Baptist (Prodromos) since the byzantine years. In the last years of the Turkish occupation this monastery reached its apogee, as it belonged to the exarchate of Pirgi - Volissos. The church has excellent conditioned frescoes painted by the well known Konstantine Katarractis in 1730. They have a naive but expressive style and a daring plurality of forms.

Pitios

After the Diefcha village we get onto the central road of Hora - Volissos. As we return to Hora another mountain road to our left heads for Kardamila, passing by **Pitios** village, one of the most important in northern Chios, possesing a medieval character.

There, above a cliff rises an uneven but imposing two story tower, surrounded by ruins of a perimeter wall. The village grows out of one side of the tower. We can see the domes and arches of the old houses, realizing that Pitios was built like the medieval houses of the south.

Going back to the central road of Hora - Volissos, we try an eastern direction to Hora.

We traverse the uncanny, desolate, bald plateau of Epos. There is no sign of life for 25km.

The dry land full of rock and dried shrub is interrupted in places by little pockets of young pines, giving a fresh breath of life to the area.

The trees have been planted by various Chian agents and other public interest organizations vying to restore the ecosystem. When the plateau nears its east border, to the left, the excavations of 1952 have brought to light the remains of an ancient fort - Rimocastro (Deserted Fort), after which the whole area was named. From the edge of this elevation, about 500m. above the sea, the view is breathtaking.

Then the steep road snakes down to Vrontados and Chios' suburbs.

Gyaliskari, a small, enchanting inlet to the northwest.

9

NORTHWESTERN CHIOS

Mt. Epos - Katavasi - Sidirounta - Metohi
Volissos - Ayia Marcella - Ayio Galas

The main road Hora - Volissos suddenly ascends on the Epos plateau. Once more in front of our eyes unfolds the immense view of Kampos, Chios and the blue Aegean Sea all the way to Asia Minor; a majestic sight that makes you think you are on an airplane. Traversing the bald plateau, the visitor arrives to Katavasi (Descent), a small village on a winding road that leads to the western shores. A little to the south is Sidirounta, a small picturesque community on a hill, from where the sea seems to sparkle like thousands of pearls under the rays of the Greek sun. Further up is Metohi a new coastal community with an attractive beach, that now develops into a tourist resort. North of Katavasi the road heads to Volissos, a place with a rich history, the center of northern Chios. This idyllic small town is built on a hill slope, below a byzantine castle that gives a romantic note to the scenery. It is said that Homer lived here. In the Middle Ages the famed general Velissarius was offered hospitality here also. The coast of Volissos forms beautiful sand beaches, some of the best in Chios. Next is Managros, Magemena and Lefkathia.

North of Limnia and Volissos' harbor lies the famous convent of Ayia Marcella, built for Saint Marcella who became a martyr and died here. The northwest side of Chios, accessible by the mountainous road that begins on Volissos, it too, has many pleasures to offer the visitor. In the village Agio Galas (Holly Milk), the very old church Panagia Agiogalousena is built in the entrance of a cave. There, impressive stalactites have been found as well as traces of Stone - Age human habitation. Nearing the north side oh Chios the landscape changes. On the way we come upon thick vegetation and running springs. The little villages stand out for their simple, folkloric architecture. The abandoned antimony mines near Keramos, give the area a different dimension. Heading towards the north shores the the the road ends to Agiasmata (Holly Waters) and its therapeutic hot mineral springs. The return road to Volissos via Potamia (Rivers) and Pispilounta village, passes by the ruins of an important medieval fortress with expanding walls, creating a nostalgic feeling for that bygone era.

Katavasi - Sidirounta - Metohi

From Vrontados' interior land we catch the road that climbs up to the slopes of Epos and traverse the desolate elevated plateau towards the west. The first village we come upon as the road descends is **Katavasi** (Descent).

For a while following the road to the south, we get to **Sidirounta** a small community on a hill over-looking the sea with a nice view. Further south is Sidirounta's seaport **Metohi** with a few summer houses and an attractive seaside.

Volissos - Monastery of Ayia Markella

The other road to the north of Katavasi takes to Volissos, the central northern village with the rich ancient history. It is said that Homer once came here to teach Lord Chios' children.

A village location caries the name "Homer's house". Thoucidides writes that here was the old Ionian city of Voliskos. Built on a slope and crowned with an imposing byzantine castle, **Volissos** impresses the visitor on first sight. Its houses restored to a large extend, have ceramic tile roofs. Narrow alleys paved with the "liladia" that is beach pebbles, give a reference point of the village. The castle, according to the legend, was built by byzantine general Velissarius, who wanted to conclude his life here after he was blinded and retired from the battlefields.

The castle had towers, turrets, cisterns and churches, though more constructions are being discovered under the ruins of the old houses.

In the middle Ages the village enjoyed great vigor and was the wealthy center of northern Chios.

In the byzantine years during the reign of Vasilios B the Macedonian (866-867) Volissos acquired watchtowers, towers, turrets and castles to defend itself against piracy. In the year 921 the general Vardas Fokas was exiled in Chios and lived in Volissos as did Michael E the Kalafatis (Caulker) later.

Gradually many royal families from Constantinople took root in Volissos, such as the descendants of Fokas, Mavros Kordatos and Kanavoutsis. Subsequently the Genoans fortified the village's defenses evenmore, by setting towers on hills overlooking the coast to control the whole area.

The watchtowers functioned up until the Turkish occupation in 1778. This small town was always neat and well taken care of; it has pretty houses and lush flower gardens.

Along with Pirgi and the islet of Psara, Volissos was part of the exarchate that alternated administratively between the Patriarchate of Constantinople and the Diocese of Chios, until it was finally abolished in 1859 and was permanently attached to Chios along with the other exarchate members.

The plain of Volissos, second largest in Chios and very fertile, used to produce the quarter of the island's total output in olive oil.

Also well known were the area's almonds, figs, legumes and cereals. In the byzantine years there was also a thriving silkworm production which supported Chios' renown silk industry.

Since the ancient years, lush vineyards produced the famous "Ariousios" wine as we learn from Ploutarchus and various Roman authors. The area is rich in minerals too; In the Turkish era a French company mined iron on Panteugenos Mt. Around 1960 a Greek company exploited the area's zinc, lead and antimony veins, but that did not last for long. Volissos was the birthplace of Saint Marcella to whom is dedicated the homonymous monastery built on a beautiful beach of the area. Author Korais describes Volissos with vivid colors in his work "Papatrehas".

Volissos, which is crowned by its Byzantine castle, is also ornamented by superb beaches.

The lace - like western shores of Volissos are forming many beaches, most of which are sandy, ideal for swimming and play with the cool, friendly water. One of them is Managros, where permanent camping for Scouts is available.

Another beautiful beach, true to its name is Magemena (Enchanted). There follow Lefkathia, Limnos with good food - serving taverns, and between the two Limnia, Volissos' picturesque seaport with fishing boats and skilled fishermen. Here is frequent caique - tranportation to the islet Psara opposite.

Further north the road ends in another pretty beach where the monastery of **Ayia Marcella** stands. The signs of her martyrdom are still discernible. Her memory is celebrated on July 22nd attracting crowds of faithful from all over Greece.

The monastery of Ayia Markella, with a fabulous beach, houses the miracle-working icon of the saint.

Ayio Galas

From Volissos, the road continues northwest climbing mount Amani, passing by the villages Pirama, Tripes (Holes) and Melanios (Black) all built in the simple and plain local style.

On the desolate mountains we come across small valleys with running waters and sparse cultivation. We make a stop at **Ayio Galas** (Holly Milk) 66km. from Hora.

Here in a cave's entrance built from the 13th c. is the byzantine church **Panayia I Ayiogalousa** (Our Lady of the Holly Milk). It has the form of a cross with a cupola in its center.

Inside the cave there is another smaller church; during the byzantine years this was a place where monks were practicing in hermitage.

The cave has access to two larger ones, decorated with impressing stalactites and not fully explored yet.

Small scale digs in 1939, unearthed pottery fragments indicating human presence in the area from the Stone Age.

Agio Galas is built on a plateau just above the cave system.

Away from Ayio Galas the road turns east,
passing through Nenitoria, Kourounia and
Egrigoro. the landscape becomes beautiful
as thick vegetation punctuates key areas.
Near the village Keramos are the old antimony
mines and in Ayiasmata, on the north beach,
run the hot mineral springs with the iron and
sulfur-containing waters that have yet to be
developed. The road concludes its circle
towards Volissos passing through small villages.
Near Potamia to the east, after Pitsilounta,
survive the ruins of a fortress with one or two
story tower, cisterns, chapel and fortifications.
The fortress has the curious name "ta Markou"
(Mark's), indicating it was part of an extended
defense plan covering a great area.
It was abandoned after the 1822 massacre.
From Volissos we get the return road to Chios
concluding the island's town.

Panayia i Ayiogalousena at the cave's entrance. ➡

Around the fragrant island of Chios there are big and small islets scattered in the sea.
In the northeast we encounter Inousses an island - complex the largest of which is Inoussa, birthplace of many ship - owners and in the west, historic Psara.
Up to the north of Chios are the islets Margariti and Strovili and north of Mesta's Limenas lie Ayios Stefanos and Pelagonisi.
To the west of the Inousses we can see the Prasonisia, in the east Pashas and southeast Patikonisos and Vatos.
West of Psara are the Antipsara and Ayios Nikolaos.
To the northwest lies Mastrogiorgis, to the northeast Prasonisi and finally south of Antipsara is Katonisi.

The islet of Ayios Stefanos with the chapel of the same name, a picturesque brushstoke of color on the deep blue waters of the Aegean, on the west coast of the island (Ayia Eirene).

ISLETS

Psara - Inousses

PSARA

Discovering the island

The visitor will very much enjoy the island's serene life, beautiful beaches and calm clear waters. In the Idyllic harbor of Psara one can find hotels and some rooms to let.
You can visit the Archaeological Museum and Paleocastro (Old Castle) built in the 15th c.

Psara island is found 44 nautical miles NW of the port of Chios to which it is connected with frequent ferry-boat transportation.
The nearest Chian port to the island is Limnia (17 n.m.). Psara is a bald island of 40 square km and population 460. Along with neighboring Antipsara and other deserted islets such as Daskalio, Kato Nisi and Ayios Nikolaos they form a small island group.

History

In the ancient era the islet was known by the name Psira. Its history's glorious pages though, were written during the Independence War in 1821. Psara, behind Hydra and Spetses, was then the third naval power in Greece and one of the first islands to revolt against the Turks.
Its fleet captained by the notorious torch-bearers (bourlotierides) Kanaris, Papanikolis and Pipinos had sowed fear and terror in the Turks' ranks. In 1824 the Turks decided to destroy the island and attacked with 140 ships and 14000 Janissaries. A hard yet uneven battle ensued, with the Turks winning and occupying the island.
Those who escaped with Kanaris went to Evia where they later established the community of Nea (New) Psara. Many preferred to die heroically by exploding the island's munitions depot. The rest were massacred or taken to be sold before the island was put to fire.
The destruction of Psara reverberated among the Philellenes and sparked national poet Dionysios Solomos to write his famous poem that begins:

> "On Psara's range now black like coal
> Glory was walking alone and forlorn"

Psara waited until 1912 to be reunited with Greece.

In the north, built on a slope of Profitis Ilias - the island's highest peak (530m.), is the chapel of Kimisis tis Theotokou (Virgin's Dormition). It contains a interesting library with many books, some of them printed in old Venice.

The historic Psara.

When the sun sets, from Chios' port if you look to the northeast, you can see some distant lights glowing above the sea's surface.
This is the islet of Inoussa; you can take a better look at it from the ferryboat on its way to Mytilene. You can even make out its white, well-built, little houses.
In the summer the islet seems to be very busy. That is the season when the Inoussian merchant-mariners - many of them ship-owners flock there for their vacations. For the visitors who wish to enjoy swimming in its little coves, their chances to stay on the island are restricted to the capacity of a small hotel.
Next to Inoussa are many more unpopulated islets creating the Inousses Group with a total area of 14 sq.km. and population 500.
The distance from the port of Chios is 9n.m. and there is daily transportation by ferry-boats.

History

The island's strategic position in the middle of the straits formed could not escape the attention of the Venicians and Turks who used it as a naval base. Periodically, the same did the pirates, who named the area for centuries.

Discovering the island

The island's only community has the status of municipality. It boasts for its many new and old "captains' mansions".
There are also interesting churches and chapels as well as a Museum of Naval History.
Three km to the northwest lies the monastery of Evangelismos (Annunciation).
Also worthy our attentionis the chapel of Zoodochos Pigi (Life - Giving Spring) on the islet of Pasha nearby.

Inousses.

Useful information

Chios is developing her tourist industry, preserving at the same time her folklore, natural environment and laid -back nature.

Today the visitors' stay is undertaken by medium sized hotel units most of them aggregated in the eastern coast, the city of Chios, Vrontados and Karfas - a very modern resort fulfilling all expectations for confortable vacations.

Traditional hostels are also available - the mansions of Kampos, inside intoxicating flower gardens.

In most of the island's villages especially the coastal ones, apartments and rooms to let are always available. Visitors can also stay in the traditional houses of the mastic villages or other villages of the interior.

The sea is friendly awaiting to welcome all in her blue, transparent, cool water. The beaches are literally countless; big or small, pebbled or sandy, deserted or cosmopolitan, everyone of them has its own special beauty and grace.

For example, Mavros Yialos and Foki in the south, are impressive with those pitch-black pebbles and dark waters.

South of the city stretches the huge beach of Karfas, next to Megas Limnionas, the island's two of the most popular beaches. Further down is the picturesque Katarractis and south of it opens the infinite sand beach of Komi, next to Mavros Yialos and Kato Fana.

In the touristically less developed west side, there are especially beautiful and quiet sand beaches, ideal for fishing and swimming.

These are Ayia Irini, Lithi, Elinda, Managros, Limnos and Ayia Marcella near Volissos, to name a few.

Northwest of the city in Vrontados, operates the Lo beach, one of two organized ones, offering all facilities needed by the modern bather and marine sportsman.

Kallimasias unique cloth-dolls.

North of that we see many attractive small coves, such as Kardamila and Nagos the lush valley with a pebble beach.

These are only some of the island's superb beaches, if you do not happen to discover one by yourself.

If you are one who likes to explore, especially the tracks of bygone romantic eras, Chios has many interesting corners where you will find fulfillment.

In the most coastal areas, you will find fish taverns serving just-caught fish and seafood along with numerous oriental and Greek delicacies, accompanied by ouzo and wine.

Do not forget to try the famous Chiot desserts, spoon sweets, lemon blossom, bergamot and rose flavourings, not to mention the local products made with mastic: Turkish delight, mastic-flavoured sweets, pasteli made with honey and sesame seeds, and fresh marzipan.

You should also try the famous Myrovolos soaps and toothpaste made with mastic. These make great gifts too.

And if, after all this, a shopping trip seems like a good idea, Chios has some of the best places to shop. You can buy from designer labels to local embroideries in the stores along Aplotaria Street, whilst the roads around the waterfront have many souvenir and gift shops.

And as the day begins to darken, the nightlife Chios has to offer is as equally appealing. There are many cafes, ouzo bars, restaurants, pizza places and bars along the waterfront in Chios town.

At Kontari, a little to the south of the town, much enjoyment is to be had until the small hours in the live music clubs. A little further, in the cosmopolitan Karfa, the evenings are also packed. Delightful concerts are staged below the castle and there is an open-air summer cinema in the Municipal park.

Chios has much to offer every visitor. Wonderful virgin beaches, remarkable architecture from previous centuries, history, nightlife. It is a friendly, sweet, dizzying and unique island. Experience Chios and enjoy a true holiday.

How to get

By air

There are frequent daily flights from Athens to Chios (35-40') throughout the year. The airport is 3 km. from the center of the town. Information: Olympic Airways, Athens (tel. 210-9666666). Olympic Airways Chios (tel. 22710 - 24514), Chios airport (tel. 22710 - 23998).

By Ferry Boat

There are daily departures from Piraeus to Chios throughout the year. The distance is 153 nautical miles and the journey last 5 - 8,5 hours according to the ship. Information: Harbour Master's Office, Piraeus (tel. 210 -4114785, 4172657), Agencies Piraeus (tel. 210-4177453, 4179822, Harbour Master's Office, Chios (tel. 22710-44433-4). NEL Lines (ferries): Agency 1.: 22710-41319 . Agency 2.: 22710-23971 MINIOTIS LINES: 22710 24670

Chios is also connected:

By air with Thessaloniki and Lesbos. Information: 22710 - 24515. By ferry boat the island is connected to Samos, Kalymnos, Kos, Rhodes, Kassos, Karpathos, Chalki, Siteia, Limnos, Alexandroupoli. By steamship Chios is connected to Thessaloniki and Kavala. Information: Harbour Master's Office, Chios (tel. 22710-44433-4).

To the surrounding islets and Turkey:

There are daily ferry boats to Oinousses. To Psara from Chios and Volissos. There is a daily schedule for Cesme, Turkey. Information: Harbour Master's Office, Chios (tel. 22710-44433-4).

Useful telephone numbers in the Town of Chios:

Harbour Master's Office: 22710 - 44433-4
Police: 22710 - 44426
Tourist Police: 22710 - 44427
Fire Department: 199, Tourist Office
Municipality of Chios: 22710 - 41389, 44344
Hospital: 22710 - 44303-5.

Texts: L. XEROUTSIKOU, G. DESYPRIS
Artistic Editor: NORA ANASTASOGLOU - ANGELIKI SGOUROU
Photographs: D. KOLIOPANOU, P. SPYROPOULOS, K. STAMOULIS,
A. TSARABOPOULOS, Archives: M. TOUBIS S.A.

Production - Printing: M. Toubis S.A.